Welcome To
REDROCK CANYON TERRITORY

AN
OLD WEST RESORT,
MOVIE RANCH,
ENTERTAINMENT PARK, AND
OPEN-AIR LIVING HISTORY MUSEUM.

RedRock Canyon Territory Is A Cultural, Historical, And Educational Museum Of The American West And A Tribute To The Great American Western.

BLUEPRINT FOR A HISTORICAL PARK

A DESIGN CONCEPT BY DON KIRK
ILLUSTRATED BY THE AUTHOR

DC NO. 1972-92

1996 Revised Edition

Copyright © Don Kirk 1992, 1996

Material in this book that was previously copyrighted:
"Don Kirk Art Prints", Copyright © 1980 by Donald Keith Kirk
"Steam Locomotives Volume One", Copyright © 1990 by Donald Keith Kirk
"The Age of Steam", Copyright © 1992 by Donald Keith Kirk

All rights reserved. No part of this book may be reproduced or transmitted in any form or by any means, electronic or mechanical, including photocopying, recording, or any information storage and retrieval system, without permission in writing from the publisher.

Published by
SWEETWATER STAGE LINES
An imprint of

THE OLD WEST COMPANY™

5118 Village Trail, San Antonio, Texas 78218

ISBN: 0-9654341-0-9

Printed in The United States of America

SECRECY AGREEMENT

The undersigned, in consideration of the disclosure to be made to it, agrees, that it will not make any commercial or other use of and shall hold secret all information conveyed to or acquired or learned by it from Don Kirk or The Old West Company™ of San Antonio, Texas (hereinafter referred to as the author) pertaining to a design concept for an Old West Resort described herein and conceived and developed by the author and shall not disclose to third parties such information or the interest of the author therein unless and until such information or the interest of the author therein becomes known or available to the public through no fault of the undersigned: provided there shall be no responsibility to keep in confidence information previously known to the undersigned or lawfully acquired by it from a source other than the author.

_____
DATE

_____
NAME OF INDIVIDUAL OR COMPANY

BY: _____ / _____
           NAME   TITLE

BLUEPRINT FOR A HISTORICAL PARK

COPYRIGHT © DON KIRK 1992, 1996
ALL RIGHTS RESERVED

COPY # _____

This proposal contains proprietary information and is the property of *The Old West Company*™.

It is presented to _____ for his exclusive use.

This proposal may not be copied, quoted, or distributed to any individual not employed full time by the above named individual or company without the express written consent of *The Old West Company*™.

The Old West Company™ reserves the right to collect all proposals at any time.

PREFACE

"When the legend becomes fact, print the legend."
— *The Man Who Shot Liberty Valance*, 1962

In the following pages, the reader will find a plan for a historical park that embodies all the spirit and flavor of the roaring frontier West. It is a fantasy adventure encompassing a Western myth founded on Western fact.

DEDICATION

To all those who love the "Old West" and to my parents, Sam and Mildred, for their unerring faith in my talent and abilities to someday pay off.

ACKNOWLEDGMENTS

Feedback from people you trust always enhances one's work so I want to give special thanks to those who read my rough draft in 1992 and gave me their suggestions for improvement, and enthusiastically encouraged me to finish the work. Thanks go out to Jo Hames, Michael Smith, Laura Joann, Jeanette Weems and Pleas McNeel. I also want to thank my brother Douglas Kirk who has supported the idea since its inception.

ABOUT THIS EDITION

Demands for more copies of *RedRock Canyon Territory* (the first edition was limited to 25 copies as a proprietary business concept) has led to this **1996 revised edition** which includes additional material written in 1993 for a "Book II" about R.R.C.T. and material originally produced in 1994 for *Whistlestop, Texas* a concept for a nineteenth-century Railroad Town. A few items in the appendix come from the *OldWest Online* Internet Web site, written by the author in 1995.

All drawings and photos in this proposal were created by the author, some of which have been previously copyrighted. **All Rights Reserved**.

— Don Kirk, San Antonio, Texas, 1996

TABLE OF CONTENTS
RedRock Canyon Territory

PART I: OVERVIEW

INTRODUCTION I-3
SIGHT, SOUND, SMELL & TOUCH I-5
A MULTI-USE PARK I-7
IN THE BEGINNING I-9
OVERVIEW I-11
THE TERRITORIAL MAPS & PHOTOPLATES I-14
THE TOWN AESTHETIC: BASIC PARAMETERS I-17
PARK TRANSPORTATION I-21
FIRST STOP: THE DEPOT I-25

PART II: THE MAIN TOWN

THE TOWN OF WAGON WHEEL GAP (Cattle Town) II-3
LIVE ENTERTAINMENT at W.W.G. II-5
MUSEUMS & EXHIBITS at W.W.G. II-13
FOOD & REFRESHMENTS at W.W.G. II-21
OVERNIGHT ACCOMMODATIONS at W.W.G. II-23
WORKING CRAFTS & RETAIL SHOPS at W.W.G. II-25
INFORMATION & ASSISTANCE at W.W.G. II-29

PART III: THE VILLAGES

DEAD HORSE CANYON MINING DISTRICT
    (Tincup Mining Camp and Mining Company) III-3
DIABLO (Mexican Village) III-11
JACKRABBIT FLATS (Ghost Town) III-17
FORT CARSON (Frontier Outpost) III-21
THE BROKEN SPUR (Cattle and Horse Ranch) III-25
HEAMMAWIHIO (Indian Encampment) III-30

PART IV: THE RAILROAD

WESTERN RAILROAD ENTERTAINMENT IV-3
ON-THE-TRAIN ENTERTAINMENT IV-5
THE ENGINEHOUSE MUSEUM IV-9
SPECIAL EVENT RUNS On The W.W.G.,T.&D. IV-13

PART V: THE REST OF THE STORY

SPECIAL EVENTS IN THE TERRITORY V-3
RESORT ASSETS (Western Themed Resort) V-7
MOVIE RANCH ASSETS (Western Movie Location) V-9
PARK ENTRANCE (Services, Admissions, Maintenance) V-15

INFRASTRUCTURE		V-19
SITE SELECTION		V-25
IN CONCLUSION		V-29
ABOUT THE AUTHOR		V-31

PART VI: THE APPENDICES

A:	TOWN BUSINESS SUMMARY	VI-3
B:	PARK PARAMETERS	VI-7
M1:	MARKETING STRATEGY	VI-11
M2:	GUEST INFORMATION BROCHURE	VI-15
M3:	A MAGAZINE STORY	VI-19
M4:	A RADIO AD	VI-23
M5:	SPINOFFS	VI-25
T1:	HISTORICAL WESTERN FILMS	VI-27
T2:	WESTERN MOVIE DIRECTORS	VI-28
T3:	WESTERN STARS	VI-30
T4:	OUTLAWS, GUNFIGHTERS & LAWMEN	VI-31
W1:	THE CODE OF THE OLD WEST	VI-32
W2:	TELEVISION WESTERNS	VI-33
W3:	TOP WESTERN MOVIES	VI-35
W4:	WESTERN MOVIE TRIVIA	VI-38
W5:	QUOTES FROM WESTERNS	VI-40
W6:	WHY THE OLD WEST?	VI-41
G1:	GLOSSARY OF ARCHITECTURAL TERMS	VI-44
G2:	GLOSSARY OF MOTION PICTURE TERMS	VI-45
G3:	GLOSSARY OF MINING TERMS	VI-47
G4:	GLOSSARY OF RAILROAD TERMS	VI-48

REDROCK CANYON TERRITORY © DON KIRK

PART I: OVERVIEW

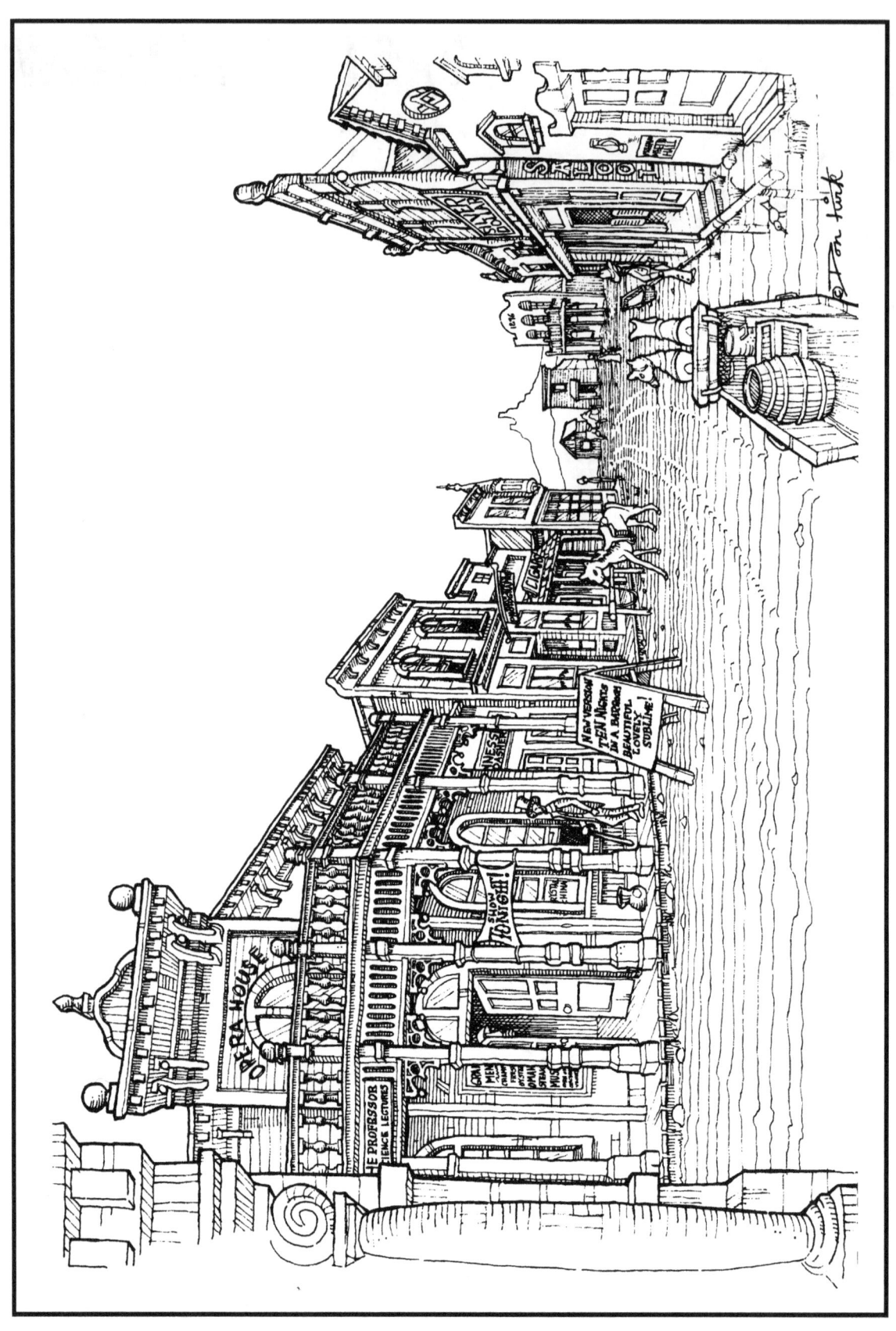

LOOKING DOWN FRONT STREET IN WAGON WHEEL GAP

INTRODUCTION

"Eastward I go only by force;
but Westward I go free."
— Henry David Thoreau

RedRock Canyon Territory is a dream world for western movie buffs and fans of the American West. Here they can take a trip to the past and explore all aspects of western popular culture through museum exhibits, books, films and entertainment of the period. The grandeur of the barren landscape and the rustic, weathered towns of **RedRock Canyon** envelop the guest in western fact and folklore. Guests step through the silver screen and find themselves inside the world of the Western movie.

RedRock Canyon Territory is a tribute to the fantasy that is the American Western and it is a tribute to the western film stars and movie makers who turned American history into a mythology equal to anything the Greeks ever produced. It's also an educational adventure for the serious study of the American West. It's and open-air living history museum unmatched anywhere in the world.

RedRock Canyon Territory takes us into the lives of the people and their times, bringing to the guest the "feel" of the Old West through the sights and sounds of a living frontier community.

RedRock Canyon Territory is a historical park that is true to the era. Employees perform "First-Person Impressions," dressed in carefully researched period clothing. They are seen to carry on the daily routines of the hardworking westerner.

RedRock Canyon Territory tries to capture the essence of the American West and the legend spawned by a frontier experience unique in the history of the World.

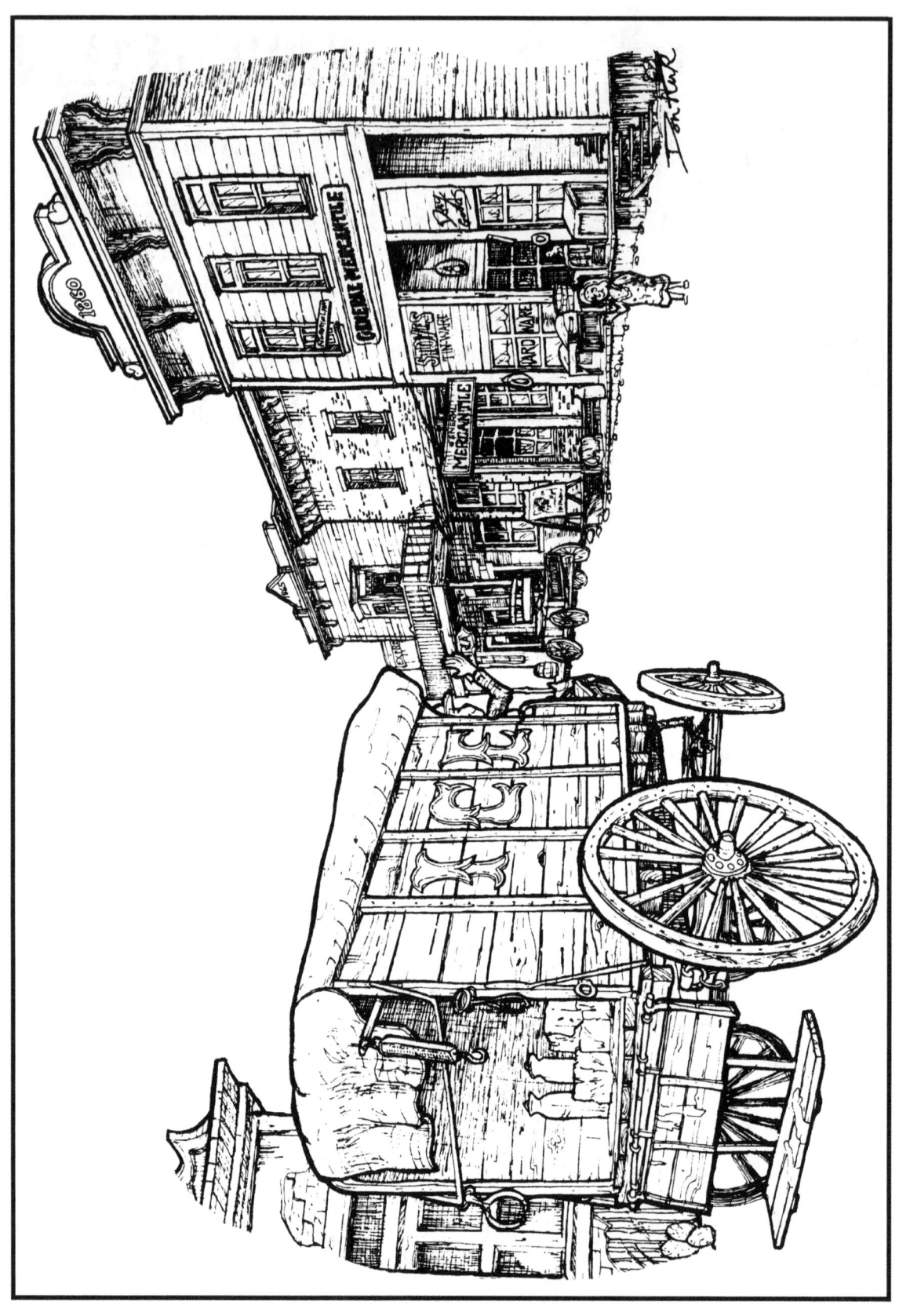

A REPRIEVE FROM THE FAST PACE OF TODAY

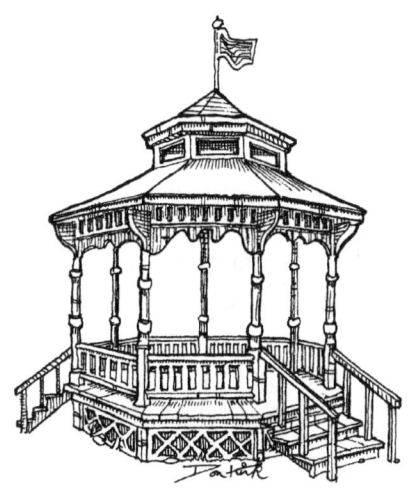

SIGHT, SOUND, SMELL & TOUCH

"Head 'em up! Move 'em out!."
— Eric Fleming, *Rawhide*, 1968

Everything is done in *The Territory* to make it easy for the guests to suspend reality and enjoy this other world of the past; to live in the Old West for a brief time and enjoy the sights, sounds and smells of a mystical period in our history that ended less than 100 years ago.

>**Experience the pleasing sight** of things built of materials in harmony with the land: wooden bridges and boardwalks, adobe and stone buildings. See the mechanical genius of the time: a water wheel and flume to move water, and ceiling fans run by fascinating cables and pulleys. Experience life before the industrial revolution, when people could understand their machines and make the repairs themselves.
>
>**Experience the sounds** of a team of horses as they pull a buckboard through town: slapped leather, clopping hooves and rattling trace chains echoing off the buildings. Hear the magical sound of the school bell clanging in the distance.
>
>**Experience the aroma** of fresh baked goods emanating from a main-street cafe, the irritating stench of coal smoke from the blacksmith's shop, the sweet smell of mesquite burning in a pot-bellied stove, the stinging scent of hay in the livery stable, and the obnoxious odor of cheap perfume coming from a boisterous saloon.
>
>**Experience the touch** of rough, weathered wood; cold, hand-forged iron; warm sand underfoot and the heat of the sun. Feel the comforting warmth of a wood fire burning in a pot-bellied stove.

RedRock Canyon will be a reprieve from the fast pace of today's society. No cars, no traffic, no television news. Life in *The Territory* is slower and a relaxed pace is encouraged. There's time to sit and watch a melodrama play, time to talk while eating "down-home" cooking, time to sit on the boardwalk and watch the people go by.

RedRock Canyon is a social community; a place for western buffs and fans to go, to sit back and "soak up" the Old West. It's a place where they can relate to others with the same interest. It's a place for sharing ideas and passing on "Old World" crafts from generation to generation.

RedRock Canyon is a place where the guest can participate in the "show" and not just be an observer. The guest is placed INSIDE the environment and can react with it.

A genuine Old West flavor is recreated with cacti, gunslingers and tortillas; with horseback-riding trails winding through acres of mesquite, with adobe cafes lit by kerosene lanterns serving bordertown cooking, with jackrabbits and deer scurrying across one's path at every turn, and with cowboys singing around crackling campfires.

The past is brought vividly to life. Families can stroll and picnic. They can experience the quiet solitude of the wide-open outdoors where the slightest breeze massages the soul. They can hear the plants struggling to survive, feel the heat from the sun and smell the sweetness of cactus flowers.

RedRock Canyon Territory is a living-history-styled recreational park. There are no plastic, glitzy state-of-the-art rides that are costly, computer-generated fusions of Hollywood special effects and old theme park rides. There are no bright, freshly painted buildings, asphalt covered streets and "Coney Island" games. There are no plastic and paper cups, and no gift shop signs.

A MULTI-USE PARK

"No man can really understand our country, and appreciate what it really is and what it promises unless he has the fullest and closest sympathy with the ideals and aspirations of the West."
— Theodore Roosevelt

RedRock Canyon Territory is a melding of several basic types of parks, carefully interlaced in a way that will allow them to reinforce each other.

ONE: *RedRock Canyon* is an **OPEN-AIR MUSEUM** showcasing nineteenth-century architecture, antiques and living history recreations of life in the American West.

TWO: *RedRock Canyon* is a **MOVIE RANCH** with all of the resources for making Westerns: interior sets, a soundstage, a props and wardrobe department, carpenter shop, horses, cattle and wagons.

THREE: *RedRock Canyon* is a **RECREATIONAL PARK** with live entertainment, restaurants and gift shops. These activities are integrated into the fabric of the "authentic" old towns in such a way as not to detract from the other goals of the park.

FOUR: *RedRock Canyon* is a **GUEST RANCH** where you can sit around a campfire and sing cowboy songs, go on a trail ride into the "wilds", eat chuckwagon cooking, and participate in an original, 1850's-styled rodeo.

FIVE: *RedRock Canyon* is an Old West **RESORT** and **RETIREMENT COMMUNITY** for anyone who loves the West and wants to participate in its preservation through teaching, crafts and research.

Auxiliary to these five main categories are the support activities found at any resort, except that at this park, they are designed to be a part of the total experience and are completely "in-character" with the major attractions.

ONE: Overnight accommodations of nineteenth-century design are found in the towns and villages of *The Territory* and are a part of the whole experience. Even the campsites are set in period environments.

TWO: A steam railroad and stagecoach line tie the Old West towns of *The Territory* together and provide for the commerce and **transportation** of guests just as it occurred in the American West.

THREE: *RedRock Canyon* is the headquarters for **living history associations**, entertainment troupes, barbershop quartets, gunfighter groups, American history historical organizations and any organization, non-profit or otherwise, that promotes, records and studies the American West and the Western movie of fact and legend. Organizations based in *The Territory* must also contribute to the goals of the park. Office space and performance areas are provided to meet their needs.

FIVE: *RedRock Canyon* is a **conservation area** similar to a national or state park, preserving the plants and animals in *The Territory.* They are a natural and integral part of the western experience. Gila monsters, desert rats, scorpions, spiders, rattlesnakes, jackrabbits and vultures are part of the folklore.

SIX: Food and refreshments using **AUTHENTIC** recipes and presentation methods are provided throughout *The Territory* at small cafes, hotels, ranches, restaurants and street vendors.

VISITORS CENTER R.R.C.T.

IN THE BEGINNING

"Life's a western movie,
and then you ride into the sunset."
— Don Kirk

RedRockCanyon Territory is a dream long held by DON KIRK, a consummate westerner in work ethic and ideal. Reprinted below is an article written by him in 1972. At that time his concept for a western-themed park was called "Arizona Territory." It's the first concrete evidence of his dream:

ARIZONA TERRITORY PRESS RELEASE

With a painted desert for a backdrop and a cast of outlaws and lawmen, **Don Kirk Enterprises** *will open an* **Old West** *Entertainment Center in Arizona just 12 miles outside of Tucson that could very well be called an "open air" museum because of its apparent authenticity and attention to detail. Three picturesque frontier towns spread miles apart, connected only by a narrow-gauge railroad and the Overland stage, bring every* **Wild West movie** *you've ever seen to an explosive adventure that will stimulate anyone's* **imagination**. *There's the exciting wild gun battles and train robberies, and Apache Indian raids and high-noon showdowns. Then there's the 'everyday' activities of the townspeople: from the marshal making his rounds to the town drunk falling in the horse trough. All of them out to turn the place into a shambles and a* **barrel of laughs**. *Out on the ranch you'll find bronco bustin' and fence fixin' and even cattle rustlin'. You're in the middle of an era and with the use of only old currency of the period to buy your train tickets or cafe meal you know you're participating in the taming of the West. A* **Gold mine** *provides a breath-taking ride in run-a-way mine cars through a dark tunnel of mystery and cave-ins. You'll get a chance to see heated courtroom trials and rollicking barroom brawls, and the* **Gold Flume** *provides a sparkling trip through a gold field full of high adventure. Everywhere, there are stunning surprises waiting to lurk out at you. You'll see all the famous western types: the hunter, the pony express rider, the miner and the cowpuncher, the cavalry soldier and the prospector, the outlaws and badmen, the vigilantes and the settlers. All there as hosts to the presentation of a thrilling panoramic view of the vast and wonderfully varied land known as* **ARIZONA TERRITORY**, *where the cactus and coyotes are the only silhouettes as the sun sets in the western sky. So, jump in, the stage is leaving for the* **Old West**.

— Don Kirk Enterprises Public Relations Department, 1972

The following proposal is an expansion of this original concept. It is a basic "blueprint" for the perfect Old West attraction, but it takes the conscious effort of a management team sensitive to the goals set forth in this proposal in order to develop this unique environment into a world class resort. The next few pages will attempt to answer the questions: "What will **RedRock Canyon Territory** have to offer the tourist, the filmmaker, and the western buff?" and "How is this entertainment park different from similar attractions?"

REDROCK CANYON TERRITORY © DON KIRK

OVERVIEW

"The (American West) was adventure, was romance, was independence, was a new dimension of self-hood. What dominated all was the splendor of the landscape in its vast scale, its earth features, its colors, its immensity of sky, its rarity of air, and its spacious light."
— Paul Horgan, *A Distant Trumpet*

RedRock Canyon Territory is a collection of rustic buildings and structures laid out on over one thousand acres of virgin western land set in a valley surrounded by rugged, rocky hills and populated with the animals and plants of a desert region. *The Territory* contains those natural symbols of the West as they appear in the western movie of myth and legend: Rugged rock formations, dry creeks, small canyons and arroyos, yucca and prickly pear cacti, mesquite trees and even a few blowing tumbleweeds shape the land. Entrance to the park and the parking of automobiles is miles from the valley, out of sight, over a ridge (see Teritorial Map #0001).

The romanticism of the Old West is recreated with the building of several towns and ranches within *The Territory*. A regional **Cattle and Mining Center** of the 1870's in the Southwest is the main focus of the park and is the largest "set" in *The Territory*. Each town is carefully "art directed" to maximize visual interest and vistas. There is a mix of wood-frame, brick, stone and adobe buildings. Built on hilly, uneven ground, the Victorian false-fronted stores and boardwalks wind around and step up and down. Buildings are not lined up in straight lines but are "zig-zagged" and angled to create interest and promote curiosity. Alleyways can be explored, unidentified doors entered. The buildings vary in elevation and number of stories producing more angles, better composition, balcony views and "camera platforms" for filmmakers. Topographically complex townsites will be chosen in order to force the design of creative and unique villages. Each of the towns will have its own personality and character dictated by its siting and its suppositional reason for existence.

Three more smaller village "sets" compliment the main town and are tied to it by a narrow-gauge steam railroad, stagecoach line, wagon roads and footpaths. The **Mexican Village** with its own Spanish Mission, cantina and market plaza, is built primarily of adobe and thatched-roof construction and is designed with a south-of-the border flavor. A **Mining Camp** situated in the foothills simulates a newly-arrived "tent town" populated by miners searching for the *mother lode*. The third village sits out on the "flats" and is a run-down, abandoned, badly-weathered **Ghost Town** sparsely populated and with only one business with its doors open: the *Crippled Dog Saloon* serving refreshments to those guests who have dared to tread this far.

A Gold and Silver Mining Complex built of large, hand-hewn timbers and clad in rusting tin, sits on the "military crest" of a hill overlooking the Mining Camp. Constructed on a much-smaller-than-actual scale, it houses an underground mine ride and mining museum. It's accessed by an aerial tramway from the Mining camp.

Two ranch sets can also be found in ***The Territory***. One is patterned after a **Mexican Hacienda** with its adobe construction, walled-in courtyard and two-story main house. The second ranch is built to the specifications of a small **Cattle and Horse Ranch** set in the middle of open ranch land. Built of wood planking, sod and mesquite timbers, the ranch has several outbuildings including a barn, bunkhouse and corral.

Just outside of the main town, on a bluff overlooking the town, is the **Carson Mansion**, a ghostly Mansardian-styled Victorian home where a haunting adventure awaits anyone who dares enter the big front doors.

And no western landscape is complete without the Cavalry to protect the new settlers as they try to carve out a new beginning in a wild land. Strategically located on an important crossroads is the **Military Fort and Trading Post**. Situated against a large rock outcropping, the fort is a small compound built of logs and stone, and consists of several buildings aesthetically arranged for a multitude of pleasing camera angles. A number of living history activities are based here.

Across the valley sits an **Indian Encampment** of buffalo-hide tipis and thatched structures sitting in the shadow of a tall butte. Guests can see the reenactment of tribal ceremonies and the routine activities of an Indian tribe of the early American West.

A small narrow-gauge steam railroad traverses ***The Territory***, connecting the towns, ranches and villages of the valley. A spur line running out of the valley allows guests to be brought into the park. Numerous **trackside structures** necessary to the running of a steam railroad can be found throughout ***The Territory*** and each works as a "set" for scenes found in any western movie. Water towers, windmills, section houses, cattle corrals and railroad depots dot the landscape just as they did in the West and become photogenic subjects with a beautifully rugged landscape for a backdrop. **Stagecoach and Freight Lines** also move passengers around ***The Territory***.

A detailed discussion about the use of each town and village, and the buildings within them, will be revealed in chapters on each subject found later in this proposal.

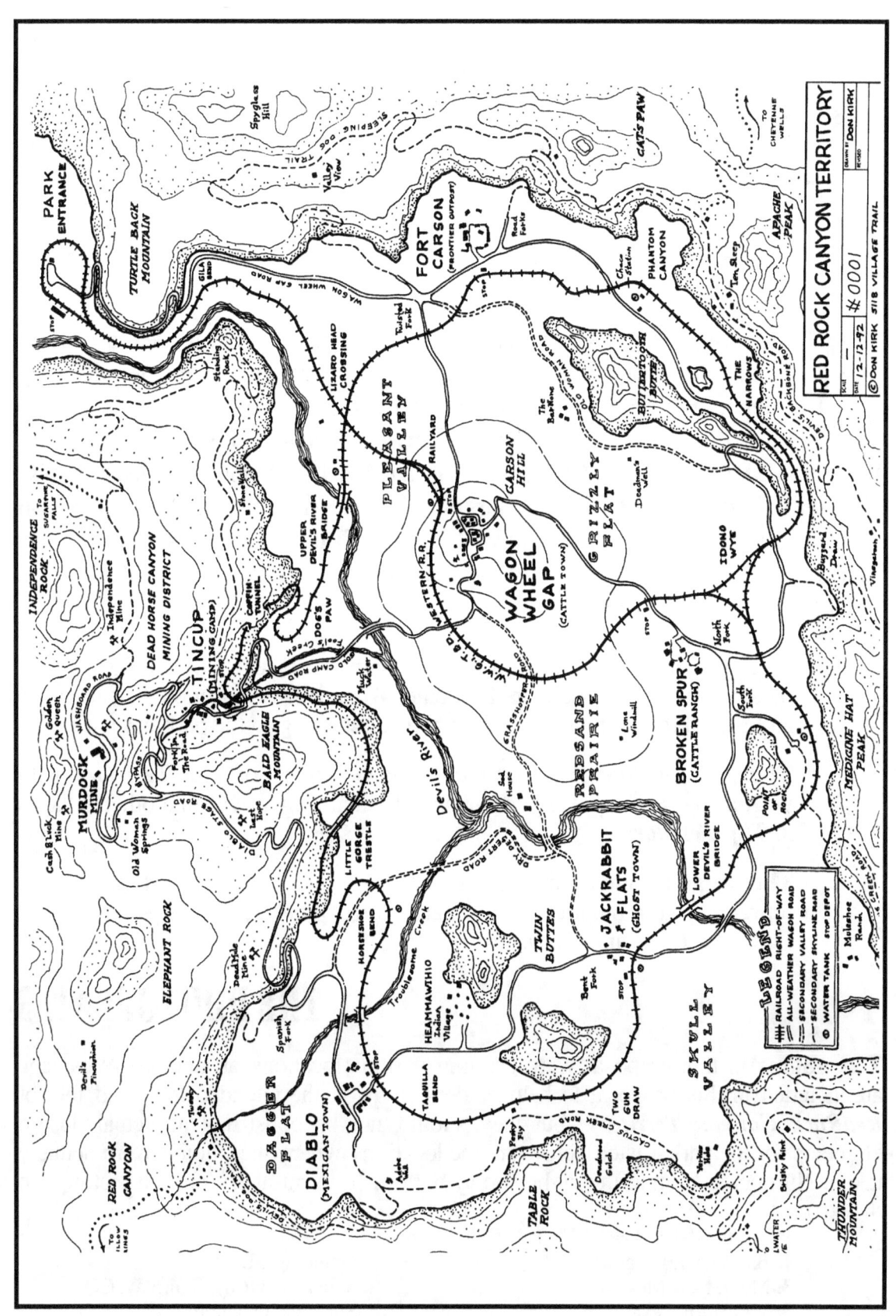

MAP OF REDROCK CANYON TERRITORY

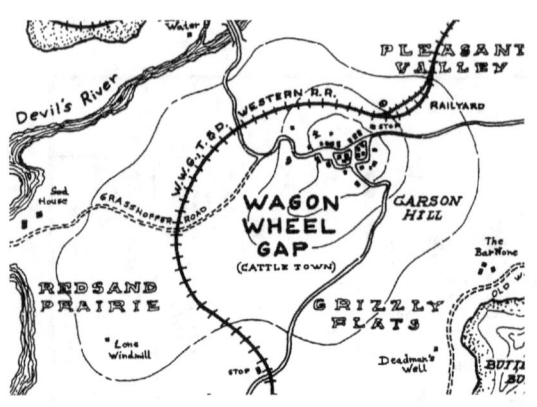

TERRITORIAL MAPS
And Photoplates

"A westerner likes open spaces."
— Kirk Douglas, *Lonely Are The Brave*, 1992

The **maps** in this proposal give the reader a general idea as to the possible layout of *The Territory*. Of course, the plans would vary depending on the site actually selected. Included in this proposal is a Territorial Map of **RedRock Canyon Territory**(I-13), and maps of *Wagon Wheel Gap*(II-2), *Tincup*(III-4), *Diablo*(III-4) and the *Dead Horse Canyon Mining District*(III-9). A larger two-page map of *The Territory* can be found at the end of the book(VI-51). **The following notes** relate to the Territorial Map (#0001) showing the narrow gauge railroad in relation to the towns and villages in *The Territory:*

> **Trains run both directions** on the main line and follow a figure-eight pattern. Arriving passengers first enter *Wagon Wheel Gap* on their train trip and pass through it a second time before returning to the park entrance.

> **The town of** *Wagon Wheel Gap* is at the "hub" of *The Territory* with wagon roads as "spokes" to connect the main town with the other villages in *The Territory*.

> **The wagon roads** that run off the map lead to the resort hotels and retirement communities of the park: *Sugarpine Falls, Cheyenne Wells, Stillwater Cove,* and *Willow Springs*.

THE PHOTOPLATES

The photos in this proposal were taken in various locations around the West and are included in this proposal to help readers envision the intended look and feel of **RedRock Canyon Territory**, but they should not be construed as actual design elements for the park. Listed below are the locations where the photos were actually taken. Numbered from left to right, top to bottom (odd numbers are the pictures on the left).

PLATE ONE: THE REAL WEST (page x)
1. Baker City, Oregon.
2. Gouldings, Utah.
3. Mora, New Mexico.
4. *South Park City,* Fairplay, CO
5. Van Horn, Texas.
6. Shattuck, Oklahoma.
7. Lincoln, New Mexico.
8. Silver Plume, Colorado.

PLATE TWO: THE WESTERN SETTING (page I-10)
1. Big Bend National Park, Texas.
2. Bodie State Historic Park, CA
3. Monument Valley, Utah.
4. Tucson, Arizona.
5. Oatman, Arizona.
6. Grafton, Utah.
7. Capitol Reef National Park, Utah.
8. Monument Valley, Utah.

PLATE THREE: TOWN CHARACTER (page I-16)
1. *RHS Studios*, Spicewood, Texas.
2. *Old Tucson Studios,* Tucson, Arizona.
3. *Buckskin Joe*, Canon City, CO.
4. Signal Peak, Colorado.
5. Bodie State Historic Park, CA
6. *Old Tucson*, Tucson, Arizona.
7. Shakespeare, New Mexico.
8. *Alamo Villlage*, Bracketville, TX.

PLATE FOUR: INTERIOR AND EXTERIOR (page I-26)
1. *Old Tucson Studios*, Tucson, Arizona.
2. Beekman Bank, Jacksonville, OR.
3. Nevada City, Montana.
4. *Old Tucson Studios*,Tucson, Arizona.
5. *Alamo Village*, Bracketville, Texas.
6. *Old Tucson*, Tucson, Arizona.
7. Craigdarroch Castle, Victoria, B.C.
8. "The Castle", Virginia City, NV.

PLATE FIVE: BUSINESS INTERIORS (page II-18)
1. *Buckskin Joe*, Canon City, CO.
2. *South Park City*, Fairplay, CO.
3. Bodie, California.
4. *South Park City*, Fairplay, CO.
5. *South Park City*, Fairplay, CO.
6. Eureka Springs, Arkansas.
7. *Buckskin Joe*, Canon City, CO.
8. Nevada City, Montana.

PLATE SIX: OLD WEST MINING (page III-6)
1. Victor, Colorado.
2. *Vulture Mine*, Wickenburg, AZ.
3. *Mining Museum,* Jerome, Arizona.
4. Tonopah, Nevada.
5. *Vulture Mine,* Wickenburg, AZ.
6. Robson's Museum, Aguila, AZ.
7. Leadville, Colorado.
8. *Tabor Mine*, Leadville, Colorado.

PLATE SEVEN: "MEXICAN ARCHITECTURE" (page III-14)
1. *Old Tucson Studios*, Tucson, Arizona.
2. *Old Tucson Studios,* Tucson, Arizona.
3. *Alamo Village*, Bracketville, TX.
4. *Old Tucson Studios,* Tucson, Arizona.
5. *Alamo Village*, Bracketville, TX.
6. *Old Bent's Fort,* La Junta, CO.
7. *Governor's Palace,* San Antonio, TX.
8. *Old Tucson*, Tucson, Arizona.

PLATE EIGHT: FRONTIER FORTS (page III-22)
1. Fort Davis N.H.S., Fort Davis, TX.
2. Fort Davis N.H.S., Texas.
3. Fort Davis N.H.S., Fort Davis, TX.
4. Mansker's Station, Goodlettsville,TN
5. "North & South," San Antonio, TX.
6. *Fort Laramie*, Fort Laramie, WY.
7. Buckskin Joe, Canon City, CO.
8. *Fort Laramie*, Fort Laramie, WY.

PLATE NINE: STEAM RAILROADING (page IV-6)
1. Embudo Station, Colorado.
2. Silver Plume, Colorado.
3. C.&T.S.R.R., Chama, NM.
4. *Old Tucson Studios*,Tucson, Arizona.
5. *South Park City Museum*, Fairplay, CO.
6. Colorado R.R. Museum, Golden, CO.
7. *South Park City Museum*, Fairplay, CO.
8. Cedar Valley, Texas.

PLATE TEN: TOWN FRONTS (page VI-2)
1. Georgetown, Colorado.
2. Leadville, Colorado.
3. Lincoln, New Mexico.
4. Central City, Colorado.
5. Silver Plume, Colorado.
6. *Old Tucson Studios*,Tucson, Arizona.
7. Fredericksburg, Texas.
8. Mogollon, New Mexico.

THE TOWN AESTHETIC
Basic Parameters

"Form, function, and simplicity. . . part of the charm of handmade houses and other structures in the West is their very crudity, designed to fulfill very specific functions, but nonetheless was marked by the personality of the builder in an individual way and few of them are exactly alike any other."

— T. H. Watkins, *Taken By The Wind*, 1977

The special and distinctive qualities of *RedRock Canyon Territory* will come from establishing clear objectives and parameters for the design and "character development" of the towns and villages within the resort. Some of those desired qualities are listed below:

ONE: The towns must be "atmospheric", having the look and feel of a living town brought out of the past, with the weather, dust and dirt of a real, out-west town situated in the wide-open spaces of virgin land. Dusty streets, dirty windows, weather-ravaged ship-lap siding, dingy dark rooms with dust-filled rays of light streaming through the windows, and creaking boardwalks. The look is drab and dingy—peeling paint, some buildings with no "white wash"—but the degree of "newness" will vary depending on the "village" being designed.

TWO: The towns are sited to "fit" naturally and aesthetically with the land and its natural features. A mining camp should be squeezed into a canyon near a creek, a fort must sit in the open with no place for an approaching enemy to hide. The towns must have a "sense of belonging" with the landscape.

THREE: All buildings must be built with the natural and indigenous materials appropriate to the area and period. Sod, adobe, wood planking (board & batten and shiplap siding), rough-hewn timbers, asphalt paper, wood shakes and clay tile roofing will be all that's visible to the guest. The type of window glass used will be appropriate to the period. Some modern construction materials and methods will be used where appropriate to strengthen and lengthen the life of the buildings. Concrete foundations can be used in some buildings, but must not be visible to the guest. Modern temperature and sound insulating materials can be used in building walls and ceilings.

FOUR: All modern conveniences necessary for the resort to function as intended in "today's world", such as electricity and plumbing, will be completely hidden from view, and used in a way that won't destroy the illusion of being in a genuine Old West setting. For example, in most buildings, the kerosene lanterns, wall bracket lights, and "gas-light" chandeliers will be electrified. The kerosene odor expected from these lights will be artificially recreated in some buildings. Modern restrooms will be hidden from sight. There must be no electrical and phone lines visible on the site, all will be buried. Buildings displaying antiques and historical artifacts will be built for temperature and humidity control. A modern, "high-tech" infrastructure will exist in the park, but guests will not be aware of its existence.

FIVE: The towns must be "broken in"; they must look as if they have been there a long time and are lived in by rugged Westerners. Some buildings look as if they are in the process of being built, others have a fresh coat of paint and new curtains in the windows, and still others sit abandoned. There is wear on brass door handles, the Marshal's bulletin board has authentic wanted posters pinned to it.

SIX: The towns must be carefully "art directed" to produce interesting camera angles and visual variety. The towns must be aesthetically and compositionally appealing from every angle—a necessity for a movie cinematographer and a joy for the amateur and professional still photographer. Numerous carefully designed "picture points" must be designed into the park for snapshooters and should be marked on site maps given to the guests. Other "professional picture points" should be provided for, and be hidden from the general guest and made accessible through "wild" pull-away walls and hidden stairs to roof and "tower" locations. To make views of the towns—as seen from distant locations—look authentic, all roofing, "backsides" and "mechanicals" must be designed to look natural in an 1800's setting. Cinematographers should have "360 degrees of view" from which to choose their shots.

SEVEN: The "aroma" of the Old West should be an important consideration to the villages and towns in *RedRock Canyon*. Little thought is given to this in other "western towns" and amusement parks. Many odors found in the villages of *The Territory* will be real, created by the living history activities taking place in the park, but the addition of others should be considered to fully re-create THE FULL DIMENSION OF REALISM necessary for a "step into the past". Most smells will be real: like the aroma of wood burning in pot-bellied stoves or the smell of coal oil from smoke-darkened lanterns, or the cooking from a quaint, side-street cafe, or the stinging scent of hay from the livery stable. The aroma of the Old West is important to the educational value of the park because many young children (and adults) living in cities and suburban communities of the "present world" will have never had such an experience. Some offensive odors will have to be controlled, such as restaurant "garbage-can wastes". But the point is that the aroma of the towns should be taken into consideration as much as any other element in the design of *RedRock Canyon Territory*.

EIGHT: *The Territory* must teach us something about the American West as it was in the nineteenth-century and it must inform us about the American art form of movie making in the context of western movies, from the first silent

"B" westerns to the present widescreen extravaganzas. There will be a mix of fact and legend, of "Hollywood art direction" and "historical authenticity" because it is understood that the myth and reality of the American West will forever be intertwined. That's the way, as a people, we seem to want it. (Note: there will be a museum building of interesting exhibits that tries to separate the fact from the fiction, if only for a brief moment in time.)

NINE: The park must reflect some genuine "feeling" for the Old West, and a concern for the preservation of this unique period in world history. The resort should promote the saving of artifacts and written records and take pride in, and appreciation of, the people who "tamed the West" and made it possible for us to have a free country with a free enterprise system of entrepreneurship unsurpassed anywhere else in the world.

TEN: Emigrants from the East trying to find a better life provided a large racial mix in the Wild West and this should be reflected in ***RedRock Canyon***. The shop owners, street venders and re-enactors would typify the period in race and ethnic background. Guests will have a chance to talk with men and women of many ancestries: the Chinese, Germans, Irish, Frenchmen, Scotts, Native Americans, and so on. The "First Impressionists" play their parts even in the gift shops. As Americans, we need to appreciate the diversity in cultures and the contributions made by all of them to the frontier.

ELEVEN: The "theme park" aspects of ***RedRock Canyon*** must not intrude on the period setting. No exterior signs shall proclaim the souvenir shops and restrooms, and no inappropriate park rides will be allowed: only those designed to blend in with the period architecture and help to educate the guest about business, life, commerce and play in the Old West. No, plastic, asphalt, concrete or any other 20th-century materials will be used as part of the aesthetic of the town, including paper cups.

TWELVE: ***The Territory*** is a living history park, not an amusement park, and as such, all rides, shows and restaurants must have some historic authenticity and should teach something about life in the Old West. Through living history associations, reenactment groups and acting troupes, realistic skits will be performed throughout the resort to entertain and educate. Authentically recreated events will occur routinely and unexpectedly in the streets and businesses of the towns: horse-drawn buckboards scurry down main street, street salesmen hawk their wares from brightly painted wagons, a cowboy drives a lone cow through town.

THIRTEEN: All vistas must be protected from encroachment by modern structures and utilities. Control of the surrounding hills up to the ridges, and possibly situating the resort adjacent to a national or state park is necessary to preserving the illusion of "stepping into the past."

More parameters for designing ***RedRock Canyon Territory*** can be found in the Appendix.

COAL TIPPLE & SAND HOUSE, CHAMA, NEW MEXICO

PARK TRANSPORTATION

"I grew up in a small Virginia town. The main line of the Southern Railway ran through it, and the heavenly roar of the trains was by all odds the most pervasive and pleasant sound of my childhood. Few of the trains stopped, but even in passing they gave off steam and smoke and a din that struck a young boy's ear like the singing of the sea. The trains started the mornings with a reveille of brisk purpose and adventure, and they punctuated the night with a sad but reassuring whistle that spoke of dangers and destinations far away."
— Caskie Stinnett, *Travel and Leisure Magazine*, April, 1993

THE WAGON WHEEL GAP, TINCUP & DIABLO WESTERN RAILROAD runs through *The Territory* connecting the towns and villages of the resort. It is a narrow gauge line on which runs authentic nineteenth-century steam locomotives and rolling stock. Passengers can embark at any of a number of depots for a thrilling and scenic ride around *The Territory*. Along the route is magnificent scenery, Indian attacks, and train robberies.

ENTRANCE INTO THE PARK. Guests to *RedRock Canyon Territory* leave their cars outside of the valley and take the train through a pass called *Wagon Wheel Gap* and enter into a serene valley surrounded by mountains. Guests are now secluded from the outside world. There are no modern vehicles allowed in the park during operating hours; movement of all restaurant supplies and gift shop merchandise is done at night or by vehicles disguised as freight wagons. Even mail from the resort is sent out by *Pony Express* riders on horseback. There are no visible signs of modern civilization, no power lines, no paved streets, no modern signs. The train ride provides the transition from today's society into the American West that was. A time machine driven by steam sets the mood for the adventure to come. Once in the park, the narrow gauge steam train ties the various aspects of the park together.

A LIVING RAILROAD. Everything is done to make a ride on the *W.W.G., T. & D. Western Railroad* a real living-history experience. The conductor, in full period clothing, punches your ticket. A *news butch* hawks his newspapers, candy, fruit, salted peanuts and soda pop and a card shark tries to entice passengers into a game of *three-card monte*. Looking through the windows, passengers see the Old West passing before their eyes: a wagon loaded with dry goods waits at a crossing, a cowhand herds a few stray cows, a ranch hand repairs a windmill. The train stops frequently to take on water or pick up a car on a siding. In this park, guests cannot be—and won't want to be—in a hurry. 1880's railroad structures all along the route (water tanks, section houses, and cattle pens) add Old West flavor to the scenery. Sitting at one railroad depot is a rough looking cowboy with a well-battered stetson, batwing chaps and a guitar. He is singing a lament about a train derailment: *"The Wreck of the Ol' 97"*. On another occasion he might be singing about the legendary *Casey Jones*. Looking out the windows of the pullman car, there are no visible signs of modern civilization; passengers see only a rugged and beautiful landscape where early frontier men and woman toiled to make a new life.

TWO SCHEDULED TRAINS. One railroad line connects the outside world to the largest town in the park: *Wagon Wheel Gap*. The other line makes a large figure-eight loop that connects the other villages, attractions and hotels in the valley. Guests can embark at any of these points and ride to any of the other stops along the line. The railroad winds and rambles through ***The Territory*** crossing wooden trestles over dry creek beds, through red rock canyons and across barren prairie. The train passes old section houses, water tanks and *jerkwater* towns made up of only three or four dilapidated buildings. A train schedule and mile marker map identify and explain the structures and features to the passengers (see Map #0001).

DIFFERENT FROM AN AMUSEMENT PARK RIDE. The typical theme park train is a shiny tin replica that "circles" the park with a view of the REAR service areas of the park. The ride provides few thrills, adventure, or surprises. A trip is more of a "rest stop" than a ride as the train spends most of its time sitting in the station waiting for passengers to load and unload. There is nothing new to be seen or discovered when taking a theme park train ride. The trip is very short and nothing is learned about railroading.

THE W. W. G., T. & D. WESTERN RAILROAD is a full-scale narrow gauge line with trains of authentically reconstructed passenger cars pulled by refurbished nineteenth-century steam engines that scale the hills, cross gorges and run along precarious canyon ledges. There are things to be seen outside the train and there is live entertainment in the passenger cars. The train is not only a part of the total Old West experience but it provides an important transportation link in the park. More about the *W.W.G.,T&D.* and railroad related entertainments will be discussed in a later chapter.

THE STAGELINES AND OTHER TRANSPORTS

THE STAGECOACH. Two stage lines, the *Sweetwater Stage* and the *Goldfield Overland Express*, provide service to all areas of the park just as it might have in the frontier American West. Guests can take the dusty, jarring ride along wagon roads to all areas of the valley. A magnificent view of the valley can be seen by taking a *Concord Coach* or "mudwagon" along the *Old Stage Road* that winds and switches back along the hills and mountains that surround the valley. Short stage hops connect each village and ranch in **The Territory** and run on a continuous basis. Sometimes a cavalry troop can be seen stirring up dust in the distance and a stage robbery by notorious outlaws is a common occurrence.

BEARD'S LIVERY & TRANSFER CO. This *wagon freighter* provides shipping and passenger services from the railroad to outlying areas of **The Territory**. Some of the wagons are used to move merchandise around the park, and others are outfitted with seats for passengers. In addition to following the same routes as the stage lines, the freight wagons go to areas in the park not serviced by stagecoach.

HORSEBACK AND MULE RIDES. Guests can also travel by horseback and mule in the various areas of the valley. One hour and longer jaunts are available at *Tincup, Fort Carson, Diablo* and the *Broken Spur Ranch*.

THE MURDOCK GOLD & SILVER MINING & MILLING COMPANY has an arial *Ore-Bucket Tram* and a wild trip deep into the *Tommyknocker Mine* (see the chapter "Dead Horse Canyon Mining District").

OLD TUCSON STUDIOS, ARIZONA

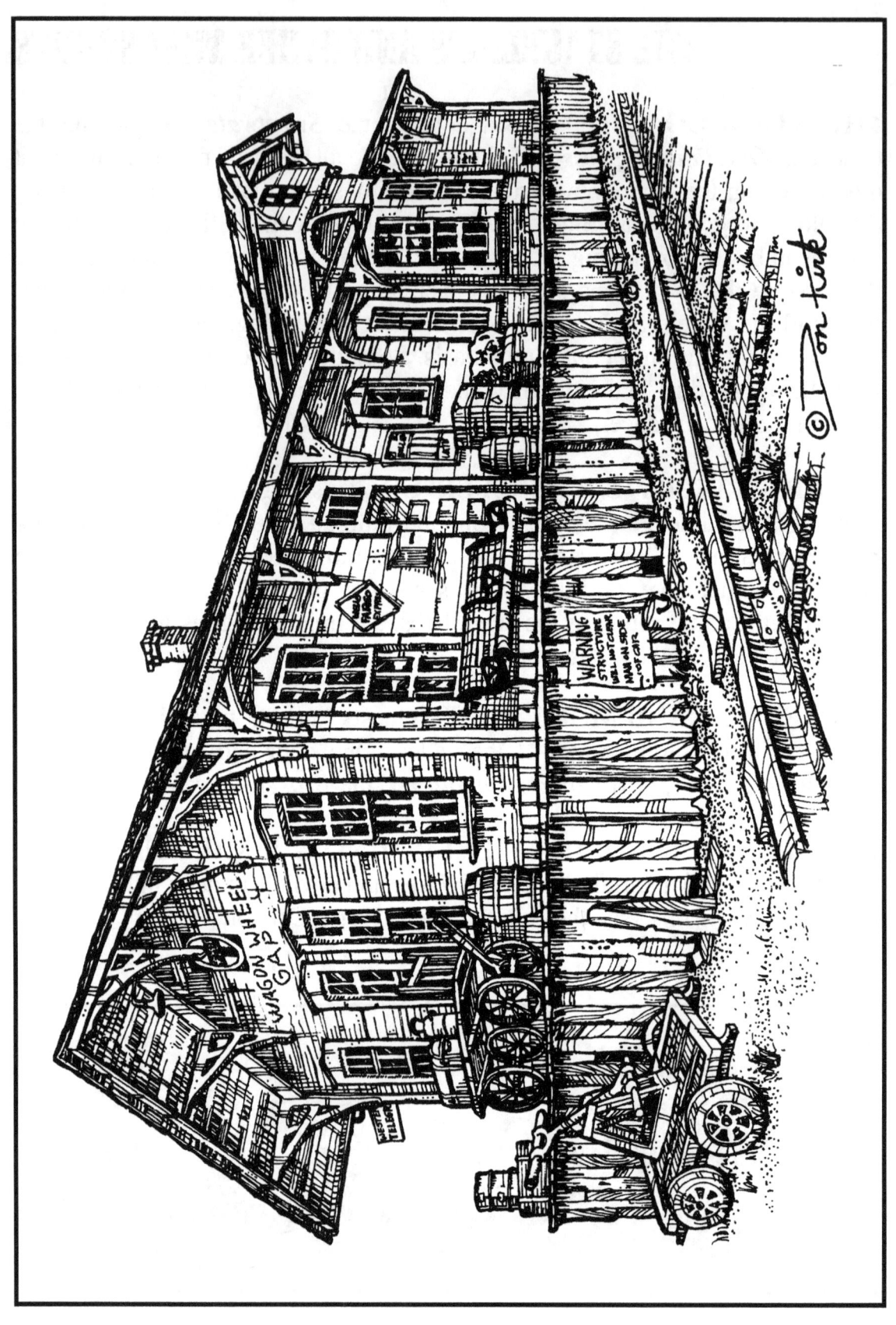

WAGON WHEEL GAP RAILROAD STATION

FIRST STOP
The Depot

"Somehow, with the loss of the depots, a vital spark has gone out of the life of the communities."
— Geoffrey Dawson, *The San Antonio and Aransas Pass Railway*, 1983

THE WAGON WHEEL GAP RAILROAD STATION is the first stop on the line. It is a bustling area of activity as visitors scurry off the train. Restaurant and other business owners are loudly calling out the names of their businesses. Horse drawn vehicles are waiting to pick up passengers and freight. On the platform sit piles of express baggage and mail sacks waiting to be loaded on the train. Chickens squawk in their little wooden crates. A *drummer* in a fashionable suit and shiny derby pulls open his steamer trunk and proceeds to hawk his wares. The steam whistle of the engine blows a harmonious tune. Visitors are witnessing—participating—in the re-creation of a bygone era and an exciting event in America's not to distant past. The *W.W.G.* depot is the most elaborate in **The Territory** with the more-expensive-to-build combination gable and hip roof with decorative trim and ornamental spires and chimneys. This one has a bay-windowed agent's office, freight room filled with crates and trunks, waiting room with wooden benches, pot-bellied stove, and train-robbery reward posters plastered on the wall. Ladies and gents restrooms are at one end of the building. A heavily loaded baggage cart sits on the platform. A red *Railway Express Company* sign hangs overhead. It is the first station new guests to **RedRock Canyon Territory** travel to, and serves as an **information center** and introduction to the park. Smaller depots in different Victorian-era styles can be found at *Diablo, Tin Cup, Jackrabbit Flats, Fort Carson*, the *Broken Spur Ranch* and other resort stops.

Now that you've arrived at the main town of *Wagon Wheel Gap* we'll discuss it in the next few chapters.

PART I-26　　　　　　　　　　　　　　　REDROCK CANYON TERRITORY © DON KIRK

PART II: THE MAIN TOWN

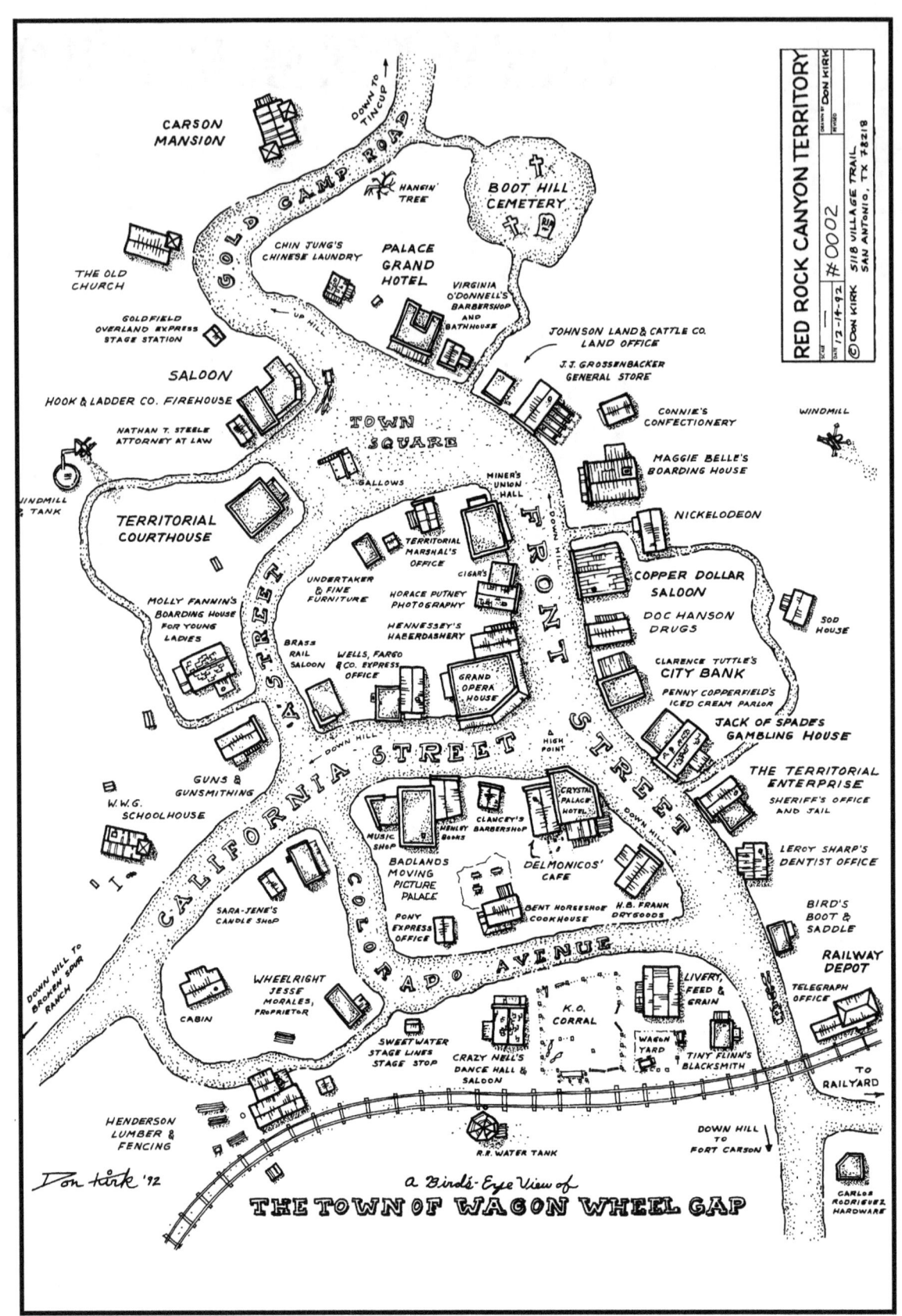

MAP OF WAGON WHEEL GAP

The Town Of WAGON WHEEL GAP

"An Easterner who walked into a western saloon was amazed to see a dog sitting at a table playing poker with three men. 'Can that dog really read cards?' he asked. 'Yeah, but he ain't much of a player', said one of the men. 'Whenever he gets a good hand he wags his tail."

— Anonymous

WAGON WHEEL GAP is a "thriving metropolis" and the pride of *RedRock Canyon Territory*. It's the cattle and mining center of *The Territory*, the seat of government and the crossroads to commerce. It's a railhead for cattle drives coming from the south and a "jumping off" point for settlers moving further West. The town is growing, having found its place in the sun. Education, religion and culture have arrived, but it still fights to put down its rough and ready past. The town is built with a variety of materials from brick on the Wells Fargo building to unpainted mesquite board & batten on the old jail. *Wagon Wheel Gap* sits on a rise in the valley with its buildings "falling off" the sides of the hill. The rest of the valley and the surrounding hills can be seen from this spectacular viewpoint. *Front Street*, the main thoroughfare, is intersected by *"A" Street* and *Colorado Avenue*. *Gold Camp Road* leads out of town to the *Dead Horse Canyon Mining District* and *California Street* leads to *Diablo*, a Mexican village out on *Dagger Flats* (see map #0002).

THE NEXT FEW PAGES describe the live entertainment, museums, exhibits, restaurants, overnight accommodations, craft shops and information services found in the main town of *Wagon Wheel Gap*.

REDROCK CANYON TERRITORY © DON KIRK

FIRST-PERSON IMPRESSIONS AT WAGON WHEEL GAP

LIVE ENTERTAINMENT at Wagon Wheel Gap

"[In the future, many] parks and attractions will be involved with the learning process and with the transference of societal and cultural values. In many areas of the world, park developers are already joint-venturing with public bodies to reclaim historically and culturally significant properties and to combine within them the elements of education, cultural enrichment, and entertainment."
— *Funworld* magazine, May 1993

LIVE ENTERTAINMENT in *Wagon Wheel Gap* takes on a number of different forms. Even though its intended to be entertainment, it tries to be historically accurate and teach the guests a bit about life in the real West. The entertainment activities listed below are only those found in the main town of *Wagon Wheel Gap,* more are described under the other villages, forts and ranches.

FRONT STREET SHOWS by the *Front Street Gang*. This acting troupe puts on unscheduled performances and sudden "outbreaks of activity" in the streets of *Wagon Wheel Gap.* The town comes alive with activity: a newsboy hawks the *Wagon Wheel Gazette*, a horse-and-buggy doctor rides through town, a circuit rider holds a noisy temperance meeting, a storekeeper unloads new dry goods from a freight wagon, a traveling salesman hawks a new iron stove that he has strapped to the back of his buckboard, and a prison wagon full of mean-looking convicts rambles down *Front Street*. Listed below are a few more examples of the type of shows performed by the *Front Street Gang:*

> **ONE:** The *Wagon Wheel Gap City Band* marches through town anytime they feel like livening up the place or advertising an evening show or special event.
>
> **TWO:** The *Front Street Gang* performs unscheduled bank robberies and high-noon shoot-outs.
>
> **THREE:** A noisy steam-driven farm tractor or a tootin' *calliope* rolls into town making a ruckus as the hawker tries to tout the new technology.

FOUR: An unkempt-looking old man walks through town with a forked stick followed by a crowd as he "witches" for water.

FIVE: At the wooden GALLOWS in the town square, the ceremony of a hanging, the event brought to an end by an outlaw gang riding into town to free the badman.

SIX: At the HANGIN' TREE players stage a "mob rule" skit that starts at the Sheriff's Office where a man is dragged from his cell and almost brought to a "quick and swift justice", saved at the last minute by an honorable, duty-bound sheriff with a pair of six-shooters.

Guests have seen these scenes played over and over in every Western; they are stuff of legend, but the *Front Street Gang* scripts often end with a twist that points out an Old West American value that should still apply in today's modern world (See "The Code of the West" in the appendix).

BUSINESSES WITH LIVE ENTERTAINMENT

The **COPPER DOLLAR** is the biggest, most boisterous SALOON in *Wagon Wheel Gap* where patrons can find food, drink and entertainment. It's your typical western saloon with a long mahogany bar—elaborately paneled with hand-carved detailing and brass foot rail, and a large "looking glass" hanging behind it. Dozens of bar bottles and decanters enameled with white and gold lettering sit in front of the mirror. Round, wooden tables are scattered about the floor, willy-nilly. Hand-made kerosene lantern chandeliers hang from the twelve foot-high pressed-tin ceiling. Shiny brass spittoons are scattered about the room. A musician tickles the keys at the player piano. At the bar, guests can get their favorite "dust cutter": *Apache Cactus Beer,* just 15 cents a glass, or *Redeye Whiskey,* so strong it'll eat rifling from a gun barrel. These drinks are actually NON-ALCOHOLIC, deliciously-flavored concoctions designed for the whole family. Live entertainment sometimes erupts in the saloon: there might be an on-the-spot "courtroom" trial with appointed judge and a jury of walk-in visitors, or a fight between dusty cowboys over a pretty saloon girl. It is said that most of western history was made inside the saloons; living history reenactments in the *Copper Dollar* attest to that fact: political candidates for the next congressional election are debated here and a verbal battle over the possible sites for **The Territory's** first capitol engage the guests in American history; bringing it alive in a way that no other medium can. The saloon was the first "public building" in any new town and it was a "stage" for gamblers and gunfighters, making it a natural place for the *Front Street Gang* to put on a show. Once a guest comes through those swinging doors, he enters into a pact with the past and he can expect to get

involved in a "barroom brawl" or a little "gunplay". A *Faro table* and *Chusa Wheel* round out the entertainment.

The **JACK OF SPADES GAMBLING HOUSE**. Gambling was a regular part of the daily lives of the people on the frontier and *Wagon Wheel Gap* is no exception. At the *Jack of Spades* guests with *Frontier Money* issued by the *City Bank* can play the original gambling games of the Old West. Games like *Chuck-a-luck, Faro, Keno, Monte, Chusa* and *Poker*. All the games are played on authentically reproduced boards, tables and wheels with period playing cards and gaming tokens. Games are played for prizes (redemption games). (Keno is like today's Bingo, Chusa like Roulette, Chuck-a-luck is played with dice in a tumbler cage, and Faro is a bit like Blackjack but with far better odds.)

The **OLD CHURCH**, with its bell tower and large room full of pews, is simple in design - a single stained-glass window has been brought in from the East. The church can be used as a "practical set" for movies and for real PERIOD WEDDINGS with the entire wedding party and guests in period clothing. The bride and groom can have their reception anywhere in town—at the dance hall or saloon—or they can take a stage to *Diablo* where they can celebrate in the plaza. Living history skits can also occur at the church and guests can climb the narrow winding steps to the bell tower for a spectacular view of the town and surrounding countryside.

The **TERRITORIAL COURTHOUSE** faces the town square with its wooden gallows as the centerpiece. Just across the street is the sheriff's office. The courthouse is a statement to all who enter its hallowed halls that justice has arrived to **The Territories**. With the help of "hangin' judge" T. A. Hawkins—who does his best to dispense justice with a firm hand—there is a chance for all kinds of excitement at his COURTROOM TRIALS. Guests are asked to participate as jury members, and you never know when the judge may send anyone who's "in contempt of court" to the jail across the square. On special occasions reenactments of actual HISTORICAL TRIALS are recreated here.

The **CRAZY NELL'S DANCE HALL & SALOON** is the place to go for a little feet stomping music. Dance the Do-Si-Do, Virginia Reel, Quadrille or any of many authentic dances popular in the nineteenth-century. Drinks are also available here. (Dances can also be held at the *Grand Opera House*).

The **HOOK & LADDER COMPANY NO. 1 FIREHALL** keeps an authentic 1860's hand pumper ready for fighting the worst fear of western town inhabitants: fire! A turned-over lantern could lead to a conflagration that would wipe out the whole town. Every evening the *Front Street Gang* recreates a battle to save the town when the Livery stable catches fire (simulated) and volunteers with red bib-front shirts pull out their pumper and hose carts and start a bucket brigade with the guests in town.

MERCHANT WAGON SHOWS are performed by the *Wagon Wheel Ruts*. The merchant salesmen who traveled from town to town were an early-American institution. Purveying small luxuries and the necessities of life, they are a reminder of the free enterprise system and frontier entrepreneurship. With their lively talk, they hauled what they could carry, goods hanging and protruding from every pigeonhole. These Eastern salesmen went west to exploit the new markets, new people and new opportunities. They tried to sell everything they could, anywhere they could get their wagons. Because these peddlers were usually loudly professing the wonders of their wares with demonstrations and shows to draw the crowd, it is a natural format for live street entertainment. Some of the individual **Wagon Shows** might include:

THE STOVE DRUMMER. With a demonstration model of a huge iron cooking stove in his small buckboard, the salesman touts the benefits of the new stove. He says it's more comfortable to use and it leaves more time for leisure. A teapot on the stove steams and whistles to punctuate the drummer's spiel.

THE FANCY GOODS MERCHANT. A colorful wagon, enveloped with merchandise of all kinds, comes into town driven by a man in "dude" dress and wearing a top hat. Strapped onto the wagon, or stuck in barrels and pigeonholes, are brooms, bolts of cloth, tinware, knives, scissors, and the like. The drummer's lively banter attracts the crowd. A small souvenir item is handed out to everyone in attendance!

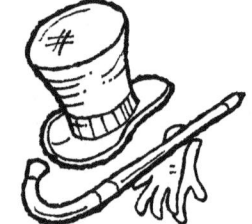

THE PATENT MEDICINE MAN. *Dr. Barthelemew Rickenbacker* puts on a spectacular show as he demonstrates the wonders of his miracle cures and celebrated remedies. The back of his wagon opens up to form a stage where he can provide entertainment to draw the crowd to his pitch: banjo music, ventriloquism, jokes, magic, or maybe an exotic animal on a leash: a monkey, gila monster, or vicious looking alligator! A confederate in the audience is instantly brought back to health after drinking the Doctor's magic elixir! But a cowboy in the audience speaks up—doubting the doctor's sincerity—and a humorous confrontation ensues.

THE WILD WEST SHOW. *Danforth Hannibal's Shooting Show and Death Defying Display of Gun Handling* puts a young cocky marksman up against elaborate mechanical targets. The marksman shoots out white discs on a rotating wheel, throws a large washer into the air and shoots through it, does fancy gun spins, and blindfolds a GUEST and stands him in front of a target. (mechanical tricks are used to create the ILLUSION of successful shooting even though the performer is using blanks in his gun.)

MELODRAMA THEATRE. The Westerners were always starved for entertainment, so when a traveling theatrical troupe came into town to present a vaudeville show or melodrama, it was a big event. A parade down main street would announce the evening's show at the Opera House, and miners, cowboys and townsfolk would plunk down their hard-earned money for an evening of lively entertainment.

The **GRAND OPERA HOUSE** is a modest building with a raised stage at one end and a second floor of balcony "boxes" on both sides. A hand-painted canvas backdrop with signs advertising the local businesses serves as the backdrop. There's also a curtain to close the show and coal-oil-lamp footlights that eerily light the performers, projecting tall shadows on the backdrop. The main floor is strewn with tables and "hurdy-gurdy" girls using their charms to sell drinks. The show might be a classic play like *"Ten Nights In A Bar Room"* or a rollicking MELODRAMA where patrons can boo the villain, cheer the hero, throw peanuts, and sip sarsaparilla. Patrons might be honored with a traveling "professor" who performs magic, ventriloquism, slight-of-hand or spellbinding lectures on philosophy or the new sciences! The *Stock Company Variety Players* try to authentically recreate the performances popular during the late 19th-century and those aren't just ON stage. A true story example will get across the idea:

> Showman Hutchinson—Billy he was called—always had a ready surprise to keep the audience happy. One evening a noisy, apparently drunken customer in one of the boxes kept shouting invective and catcalls at the performers. Hutchinson came on stage to ask that the man calm down, but the request seemed only to infuriate the shouter. With a great show of reluctance, Hutchinson sent the bouncers to eject the noisy patron. Their arrival at the man's box was followed by shouts, then the noise of a fight, and finally by a pistol shot. Horrified spectators looked up to see a man's body thrown from the box onto the stage—only to realize suddenly that the 'body' was a dummy made of straw! The whole incident was a hoax.
> — Odie B. Faulk, *Tombstone: Myth And Reality*

Everything is possible at the *Grand Opera House* and guests can expect the unexpected.

EXISTING THEATRES FOR STUDY:
Central City Opera House, Central City, Colorado.
Tabor Opera House, Leadville, Colorado, (museum).
Imperial Hotel, Cripple Creek, Colorado, (shows).

AN OLD MANSION OVERLOOKING THE TOWN

Virginia City Opera House, Virginia City, Montana.
Bird Cage Theatre, Tombstone, Arizona, (museum).
Strater Hotel, Durango, Colorado, (shows).
Wheeler Opera House, Aspen, Colorado.
Wrights Hall, Ouray, Colorado, (facade).
Granbury Opera House, Granbury, Texas, (shows).

VIRGINIA O'DONNELL'S BARBERSHOP AND BATHHOUSE. Guests can step into this authentic recreation of an 1870's barbershop and bathhouse and actually get a hot shave for 10 cents and a haircut for 25 cents (in *Frontier Money*), "Ears Washed Without Extra Charge". It's living period entertainment—feel what its like; a hot towel wrapped around your face, a sharp, straight-razor sliding smoothly under your chin as you watch it all in the large antique mirror and reflect on Clint Eastwood's "close shave" in *High Plains Drifter*. Then you can try a bath in the back room for just 50 cents. Bathe in a large antique tin tub, hot water dumped into the tub with a wooden bucket by a scruffy old man. Reservations required.

THE CARSON MANSION sits on a bluff overlooking the town of *Wagon Wheel Gap*. It's a picturesque 19th-century Victorian mansardian-styled home with simple lines and minimum decoration—painted a charcoal gray with weathered white trim. Through the large oak front doors are dusty pine floors, furniture covered with sheets, cobwebs in every corner. Fine oak wainscoting, gold-leafed wallpaper, ornate cornices, a venetian-glass candelabrum, a large marble fireplace, Brussels lace on the windows, and a grand staircase hark back to a time when the owner was the richest man in *Wagon Wheel Gap*. **Bufford Tobias Carson** founded this town and was the cattle king of **The Territory.** But that was a few years ago and times change quickly in a western town founded on sudden riches. Now the mansion has a haunting, eerie feel to it, more the appearance of an abandoned building in a ghost town. Guests who come to this home after hearing tales of the ghostly encounters by others, are entering at their own risk!

> The *Carson Mansion* is a "self exploration" type entertainment where guests explore the place on their own. The house is full of secret passageways where guests can peek through "the baron's eye" on his painting hanging over the fireplace, "run into" a skeleton of a man trapped forever by a locked closet door, and discover the basement cellar where signs of foul play are in evidence. At times the mysterious mansion comes alive with eerie sounds: footfalls on the squeaky floor above, organ music resonating through the house, a ghostly breeze suddenly moves the chandelier, glass ornaments tinkling. Sometimes, early in the morning, the strong smell of burning tallow from candles just blown out, pervades the

master's bedroom. Peek into the dumbwaiter, feel chilly air coming from somewhere far beyond this world. Suddenly the dumbwaiter car starts to move. You're out of there! Back downstairs in the Drawing Room the wood in the fireplace suddenly flames up. "Enough" you say, and out the front door you go!

The *Carson Mansion* is a simple low-tech design on a small scale. Some mechanical and electronic gags are in the mansion, automatically triggered by the guests, but it is primarily a place of self exploration. The very "hide-and-seek" nature of Victorian era homes lends itself to this "look for yourself" entertainment. A magnificent view of *Wagon Wheel Gap* can be seen from the front verandah and from the widow's walk on the roof.

VICTORIAN HOMES FOR STUDY:
Bloom House, Trinidad, Colorado.
McAllister House, Colorado Springs, Colorado.
Fulton Mansion, Fulton, Texas.
The Maxwell House, Georgetown, Colorado.
Morning Glory Mansard, Leadville, Colorado.
Hamill House, Georgetown, Colorado.
Copper King Mansion, Butte, Montana.
General Dodge House, Council Bluffs, Iowa.
Bowers Mansion, Carson City, Nevada.
Ace Of Clubs House, Texarkana, Texas.
Steves Homestead, San Antonio, Texas.
Ferris Mansion, Rawlins, Wyoming.

HISTORIC TOWNS FOR STUDY:
These legendary towns are again "booming" due to legalized gambling or a tremendous growth in summer tourism.
Virginia City, Nevada
Central City, Colorado.
Tombstone, Arizona.
Bisbee, Arizona
Georgetown, Colorado.
Cripple Creek, Colorado.
Leadville, Colorado.
Deadwood, South Dakota.
Telluride, Colorado.
Butte, Montana.
Jacksonville, Oregon.
Idaho City, Idaho.
Skagway, Alaska.
Sheridan, Wyoming.
Eureka Springs, Arkansas.
Galveston, Texas.

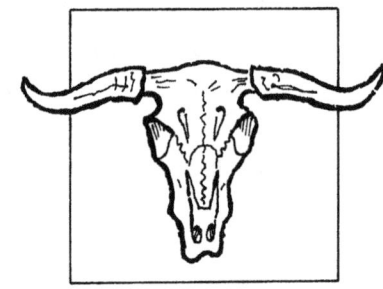

MUSEUMS AND EXHIBITS
at Wagon Wheel Gap

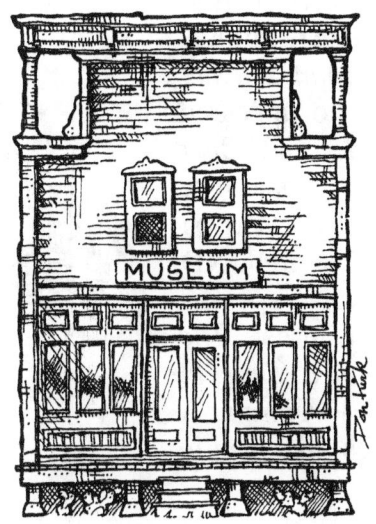

"There is a nebulous but substantial understanding that comes only on direct confrontation with what historian Brooke Hindle calls a 'three-dimensional embodiment' of history. In trying to explain the value of material objects to the study of history, Hindle says 'somehow many objects belong to the viewer and are firmly a part of his understanding of history in a way that would have been totally impossible had he never seen them!'"
- Agnesa Lufkin Reeve, *From Hacienda To Bungalow,* 1988

The entire town is a living history open-air museum and as such, buildings all over the town express historically accurate building construction techniques used during the nineteenth century. Some of the buildings are set up as "museum exhibits" and are completely furnished in original antiques, others are furnished in authentic reproductions. As opposed to the typical museum where miscellaneous items are stuffed into glass cases lined along walls with little typed cards explaining their use, and artifacts are lit by flickering florescent fixtures, in ***RedRock Canyon Territory***, the antiques are put in their natural setting and are lit by natural soft window light and tungsten lanterns. Grouping antiques together in a realistic setting (for example, shaving mugs and straight rasors in a barbershop) helps greatly to understand their use and the life style of the westerner who used them. Living history programs are devised to demonstrate the activities and use of buildings and equipment in the frontier west.

MUSEUMS

Some of the buildings are set up in a more conventional way to show and explain specific "themes" related to the American West. Others pay tribute to the Western genre movie.

> The **WELLS, FARGO & COMPANY EXPRESS OFFICES**. The MUSEUM OF THE AMERICAN WESTERN is a tribute to the makers and stars of the Western film. The history of the American Western is depicted with stories, pictures, and MOVIE MEMORABILIA. There are

exhibits about the classic western film locations like *Monument Valley, Vasquez Rock* and *Lone Pine*, and then there are **western movie superstars** like *William S. Hart, Tom Mix, Gary Cooper, John Wayne, Randolph Scott* and *Clint Eastwood*. And big screen stars who appeared successfully in Westerns like *James Stewart, Henry Fonda* and *Burt Lancaster*. Character actors have their own "walk of fame": people like *Jack Elam, Andy Devine, Struther Martin* and *Noah Berry, Jr*. Also on display are original CAMERA, LIGHTING, AND SOUND EQUIPMENT used during the early days of filmmaking. Over a speaker system, guests will hear **theme songs** from various westerns: *The Magnificent Seven, The Man with the Harmonica, Once Upon a Time In The West*, and from series television like *Bonanza* and *The Virginian*. A tribute is also made to the **musicians** who wrote the scores like *Ennio Morricone, Elmer Bernstein* and *Demitri Tiomkin*.

The **NICKELODEON** is a narrow, dark and dank room—a screen at one end—filled with old chairs and wooden benches. An old hand-cranked projector sits at the back of the room. For a nickel, patrons can see the great stars like *Lash LaRue* and *Buck Jones* in the film classics of the silent screen. As a tribute to the genre, Old-time Western "flickers" are run continuously in this movie theatre. Guests can come in at any time and stay as long as they like. Kids scurry up and down the isle during the show selling snacks and drinks. Lantern slides periodically interrupt the program with "Do Not Spit, Remember The Johnstown Flood", or "Please Do Not Stamp Your Feet, The Floor May Cave In". Besides Saturday matinee serials, the best and most famous black and white classic films will be shown: *The Searchers, Stagecoach, Shane, High Noon,* etc. (The movie house, of course, doesn't fit into the time period of *Wagon Wheel Gap* so it is placed on a side street out of camera view).

The **BADLANDS MOVING PICTURE PALACE**. A larger MOVIE THEATRE is also hidden in town that is designed to show uncut 35mm wide-screen western movies in their original grandeur, not cut up, cropped, and squeezed onto a tiny TV screen. Dressed up like a grand old 1930's movie theatre, the *Palace* will have crystal chandeliers, plush carpeting, upholstered seats, artwork on the walls and a Mighty Wurlitzer for music at intermission. Guests can see classics like the *Wild Bunch, Butch Cassidy And The Sundance Kid* and *The Good, The Bad and the Ugly*. The wide grandeur and magnificence of the WESTERN LANDSCAPE is celebrated here as much as the movies themselves. In the outer lobby is a display of some of the early, very colorful and graphic, WESTERN MOVIE POSTERS and LOBBY CARDS. (The theatre is also set up to be used for showing "dailies" by film production companies working in **The Territory**.)

The **ELECTRIC LIGHT PLANT**. A MUSEUM OF LIGHTING: The history of artificial light, from the campfire to the candle, to kerosene and gas lights to the electric light bulb. Guests will find displays about photocells, chemical light, and the firefly! All types of light are on display and in working order (ofcourse, authentic period lighting fixtures are used throughout the park). Kids can smell the odor of an oil lamp and touch the soot. They can experience the kind of light they would have had to do their homework under at the kitchen table in grandpa's day.

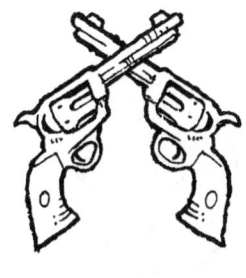

The **GUNS & GUNSMITHING, NATHAN WAINRIGHT, PROP.** is a WEAPONS MUSEUM of nineteenth-century longarms and handguns displayed in a setting that looks like a gun shop. Guests can see up close, a private collection of guns like the famous *Model 1873 Winchester* and the *Colt Dragoon* pistol. There's the Army and Navy revolvers, "pepperboxes" and "hide-a-way guns", *Remington* and *Smith & Wesson* revolvers, the *Sharps* repeater and "trapdoor" *Springfield*. The museum includes antique gun leather; holsters, gunbelts and bandoleros. A unique collection of sheriff badges is also displayed. Further back into the museum, guests can learn something about high-noon showdowns with a mechanical fast draw demonstration. The SPEEDS FINE BUT ACCURACY'S FINAL room is an attempt to explain to the guests the importance of weapons in the West and how they affected the outcome of historical events. The GALLERY OF GUNFIGHTERS showcases the famous gunfighters of legend and the type of weapons they used.

The **JOHNSON LAND & CATTLE COMPANY LAND OFFICE**. This COWBOY AND WESTERN ART GALLERY displays original paintings and art prints from well known western artists like *Frederic Remington, Charles Russell, Albert Bierstadt* and other early artists that recorded the American West before the age of photography. Modern western artists are also represented.

The **MINER'S UNION HALL**. This is the OLD WEST TRUTH & LEGEND MUSEUM: Legend or Myth—Fact or Fiction? This museum is an entertaining analysis of the Old West using demonstrations, comparative photographs and film clips to ferret out the truth about the American West. Where there really high-noon shootouts? Was there any advantage to having a fast draw? Did every cowboy wear a vest? The truth has been blurred with the myth and the museum tries to find the facts in a fun and enlightening way. Period photographs are placed side by side with stills from contemporary movies to show the differences in architecture and clothing. Manikins are placed side by side, some dressed in actual period clothing and the other in the Hollywood wardrobe—designers version. A chronological display outlines the development of clothing and shows when new "inventions" and styles were applied to clothing. When did the zipper replace the button-front trousers? When did waist belts and belt loops replace "galluses"? On the second floor is a RESEARCH LIBRARY of thousands of books about the American West and about western movies. It's available to anyone who wants to do research on the subject. The library is an enormous, high-ceilinged room with a fireplace, plush reading couches, floor lamps, glass-fronted bookcases and bearskins laid over a solid oak floor.

MOLLY FANNIN'S BOARDING HOUSE FOR YOUNG LADIES. Just "Ring Bell For Service." *Molly Fannin's* is a MUSEUM recreating a typical BROTHEL of the Old West. Prostitution was an accepted facet of frontier life. The first men in the West were usually single and were far from wherever they called home. With so few women out West it was no wonder that bawdy houses did a thriving business. Madam Molly's home is a lavishly decorated two story building with small rooms strung together by a long hallway. First names on the doors attest to the profession of the inhabitants: *Nelly, Pearl, Hannah, Cinnamon, Paulene, Virginia-Ann, Tuesday* and *Charity*. Each little room is furnished with a polished brass bed with patchwork quilt, marbletop dresser, rocking chair and the "boarders" personal things. The girls take pride in their abodes and have dressed them up with garish wall paper, fancy curtains, family photos and their favorite bric-a-brac. In addition to rooms for the ladies, there's space for the housekeeper, maid, butler, porter, and piano player! In the parlor room on the first floor, with its glass chandelier, large stone fireplace and the finest imported, red-flocked wallpaper, guests will find the finest Eastern couches, lounge chairs, upright oak piano, and an old Edison phonograph with its large "morning-glory" speaker.

MUSEUM OF 19TH-CENTURY TECHNOLOGY. Here guests will find a display of turn-of-the-century mechanical genius from a hand-cranked commercial apple-peeler to a steam-driven tractor. The industrial revolution created mechanical gadgets to make life easier on the farm, and belt-driven machines to make work easier in the factories. (COIN-OPERATED PIANOS and ORCHESTRIONS are displayed around town in such places as the saloon, dance hall, hotel and cafe. With the insertion of a *Frontier Money* coin they will come alive with captivating sounds.)

EXHIBITS

Building interiors classified as "exhibits" are furnished with both original and reproduction furnishings in order to recreate the interiors of typical businesses of the Old West. These were chosen based on their frequency of use in Westerns and their stereotypical nature.

J.T. GROSSENBACKER GENERAL MERCHANDISE is an elaborate recreation, completely stocked with merchandise of a bygone era. An antique brass cash register and a red coffee mill with gold lettering sit at the front of the store. Weight scales and a cheese slicer sit quietly on the counter at the rear. The glass-fronted counter is filled with grains, nuts, cereals and candies of all kinds. The General Store is a favorite gathering place for adults and children alike. Guests might find cowhands sitting around the pot-bellied stove playing checkers with playing pieces cut from a corn cob. Kids can buy "period" candy from the storekeeper. Pigeonholed goods cover the walls: bolts of cloth, *airtights* (can goods), one-size-fits-all shirts, groceries, drugs, hardware, clothing and liniments. Pots, pans and tools hang from the exposed rafters. Customers of the 1880's general store could also find baking soda, salt, coffee, cheese, pickled fish, vinegar, sugar, spices, tobacco, blankets, toys, magazines, playing cards, Bibles, *readers* (school books), and much much more. *Grossenbacker's* is the place to see a large collection of antiques in a natural setting.

The **SHERIFF'S OFFICE AND JAIL** is a completely furnished "practical set" with several holding cells in the back. A locked wall case holds an assortment of rifles and a large wooden desk has wanted posters and town-business papers strewn on top of it. A coffee pot sits on a small pot-bellied stove.

CLANCEY'S BARBERSHOP is a "practical set" completely furnished with original chairs, mirrors, straight razors, leather straps, shaving mugs and other sundries. The BARBERSHOP "set" is built large enough to use in filmmaking, with a "wild wall" and a room behind the large one-way mirror. (See *Virginia O'Donnell's Barbershop* where guests can actually get a shave for 10 cents and a haircut for two bits in *Frontier Money*).

DOC HANSON DRUGS has on the first floor a large DRUG STORE, shelves crammed with patent medicines, soaps, jewelry, perfumes, *trusses* (to heal what ails ya'), shoulder braces, kerosene, school supplies, cigars, soda water, and even licorice sticks. Guests can get a *sarsaparilla* from the marble-topped soda fountain. On the second floor, up the outside stairs, is the DOCTOR'S OFFICE a small "peek in the door" exhibit: a patient lays on the examining table, as the Doc and an assistant lean over him wrapping his leg in a splint. Next to the office desk sits a medicine cabinet full of odd-shaped glass bottles. A glass instrument case is lined with evil-looking surgical instruments. (The "people" are just mannequins in an "action diorama": an example of a "discovered" exhibit as guests wander the town looking into doors and windows. They are surprised by the unexpected when exploring. One discovery entices them to continue to look in every nook and cranny for something else to see or do.)

PART II-18 REDROCK CANYON TERRITORY © DON KIRK

The **WAGON WHEEL GAP SCHOOLHOUSE** sits at the end of *California Street*, with its white-washed *clapboard* siding and tall bell tower. A little playground, with a hand-made swing and teeter totter, sits to the side of the school. In the back, are seperate outhouses for the boys and girls. Inside the litle scholhouse, on the wood-plank floor, sits a pot-bellied stove and bench type desks. The American flag hangs over the blackboard behind the teachers desk. The room is "dressed" with props to make it look as if class has just been in session: coats hang on the hooks in the back, drawings are pinned on the wall, a copy of the *McGuffy Primer* lays on each students desk. The teacher's desk is cluttered with test papers.

The **LIVERY, FEED & GRAIN** is a small barn with hayloft and attached tool shed. It has several stables, a feed room and a tack room. A sign on the barn says "Keeps Buggy-Tops. Paints Buggies at Reasonable Prices". A man does what he can to make a living. The livery stable was not only a resting place for weary travelers and their horses but one could buy or trade horses and gear, and rent a buggy or wagon. Guests to **RedRock Canyon** may see the owner "haggling" with a customer over the price of a horse. The *K.O. Corral* is situated next to the *Livery*: horses, in several breeds, are kept here for the *Wagon Wheel Ruts'* entertainment wagons.

The **WAGON YARD** behind the *Livery, Feed & Grain* displays a few period wagons, but most of the wagons in **The Territory's** collection are displayed as *set dressing* in the the towns around the park. Guests will see original buckboards, surrys, freight wagons, buggies and covered wagons in appropriate areas. They are all numbered with a letter so guests can read about them in their museum literature. Only reproduction wagons are used by the *Wagon Wheel Ruts* and other reenactment groups in their skits. Other vehicles, like the stagecoaches and freight wagons, are used to move guests and supplies around **The Territory** (see chapter on "Park Transportation").

The **MORTIMER PEEL'S UNDERTAKER & FINE FURNITURE**. A sign reads: "Custom Made Caskets, Coffins and Fine Furniture". This is a diorama exhibit showing the men (mannequins) at work: *Mr. Hagy* hammering together a coffin while *Mr. Sloan* makes funeral arrangements with the next of kin. A list of business guarantees hangs on the wall: *"All pine boxes made to order, five minute eulogy guaranteed, no bad words."*

The **NATHAN T. STEEL, ATTORNEY AT LAW** is a *practical set* recreating a lawyer's office. Lawyers were important to the West, dealing with disputed land claims, descent of estates, the probate of wills, etc. The office has two walls covered with bookcases full of huge leather-backed books, a large writing desk and an oak filing cabinet.

EXISTING MUSEUMS FOR STUDY:
These are museums with a collection of original buildings brought to the site from other locations. Many contain interiors furnished in period. At some of them, costumed artisans perform daily chores and practice old-time crafts.
South Park City State Historic Site, Fairplay, Colorado.
Oxbarn Museum, Aurora, Oregon.
Chelan County Historical Museum, Cashmere, Washington.
Westville, Lumpkin, Georgia (Antibellum South).
Pioneer Arizona Living History Museum, Phoenix, Arizona.
Miss Hatties, San Angelo, Texas (bordello museum).
Boot Hill Museum, Dodge City, Kansas.
Old Homestead Parlor House, Cripple Creek, Colorado (bordello museum).

MAIN STREET OF OLD TUCSON STUDIOS, ARIZONA

FOOD AND REFRESHMENTS
at Wagon Wheel Gap

"No shooting, cutting, fighting, or loud cussing allowed, and absolutely no spitting on floor. —R. Bean, Proprietor."
—Sign in *Judge Roy Bean Saloon*, Langtry, Texas

Food and refreshment establishments are found in every town in *RedRock Canyon Territory*. Each restaurant specializes in different cuisine, making each establishment unique. Authentic, historically accurate recipes from the nineteenth century are used to prepare the menus. No plastic or paper cups and plates are used; drinks are served in glass or tinware. The patrons are encouraged to relax and spend time in the restaurants, where there's live entertainment and lots of things to see and do. Recipes and information about the cuisine is published and available to guests in accordance with the educational objectives of the park.

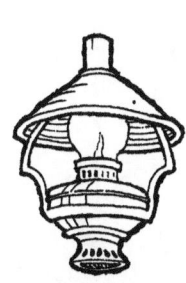

The **COPPER DOLLAR SALOON**. Ballads from an old upright piano, the tinkling of shot glasses, the shuffling of cards and the clattering of chips set the mood in the *Copper Dollar*. Guests can get their favorite "dust cutter" at the long mahogany bar: *Apache Cactus Beer* is just 15 cents a glass and a shot of *Redeye Whiskey* is two bits a shot. An if that's not to your liking, try the *Skull Bender, Stone Fence* or the *Bumblebee*, the drink with a sting. These and many other delicious non-alcoholic concoctions are available if you have the gumption to step up to the bar (real alcoholic drinks are only available in **The Territory**'s restaurants). Guests can also get sandwiches and cold cuts. A more detailed description of the ENTERTAINMENT at the saloon will be found under the chapter "Live Entertainment".

The **BRASS RAIL SALOON**. Smaller than the *Copper Dollar*, and lacking glass chandeliers and flocked wallpaper, but still serving your favorite drink, is a "side street" saloon with dingy lighting and sawdust on the floor. The only entertainment is light conversation over a game of checkers and an occasional barroom brawl performed by the *Front Street Gang*.

DELMONICO'S. Located next to the *Crystal Palace Hotel, Delmonico's* restaurant serves the finest cuisine west of the Mississippi: champagne and fresh oysters from the East and the finest steaks from Omaha. And guests will find good down home cooking: homemade bread, corn on the cob, and mashed potatoes. Dinner is served with music from a *Wurlitzer* orchestrion. A small "period set" kitchen is on display in an adjacent room. A fenced in area at the back of the hotel houses chickens and a vegetable garden (not actually used today as the source for the cafe food).

The **BENT HORSESHOE COOKHOUSE** serves American cowboy, hickory-smoked, "Bar-B-Que" and hamburgers. Cooked in a closed pit is beef, pork, chicken, buffalo, elk and venison served with all the trimmings: potato salad, coleslaw and pickles. For dessert, try pistachio icecream, hot mince pie, French pastry or chocolate eclairs. While they devour the "fixins", guests might hear some real hot fiddle playing.

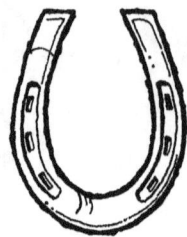

PENNY COPPERFIELD'S ICED CREAM PARLOR. Here guests will find old-fashioned icecream just like grandma used to make. The parlor serves various, sweet and cold, historically accurate, icecream concoctions in vanilla, peach and pistachio flavors. Guests can also get genuine *Sarsaparilla* (tastes kind of like root beer) and rock candy, barley pops, licorice sticks and caramel twisters!

CONNIE'S CONFECTIONERY. Walk into a wonderful aroma of fresh baked goods: bread, cookies, pies, pound cake, funnel cake, apple fritters, and apple dumplings, all prepared from original recipes of the nineteenth century. Patrons will also find a wide variety of tasty "period" candies: Peppermint drops, molasses taffy, lemon drops, and buttermilk candy.

STREET VENDERS. *The Territory's* "moveable food operations" are divided into four categories:

ONE: JUICE AND LEMONADE STANDS serving cold drinks like iced Mango Tea and Rio Grande Lemonade.
TWO: ICE CREAM STANDS serving flavors like mango-peach and Pistachio.
THREE: CONFECTION WAGONS serving sopapillas, funnel cakes and bizcochos.
FOUR: MEXICAN FOOD CARTS serving cheese nachos, hot border chili, grilled corn on the cob, beef-jerky, and giant "cowboy" cookies.

A sampling of Old West Recipes might include Wild Card Chili, Red River Bean Soup, Chicken and Dumplings, Way Station Beef Steak, Sourdough Steak, Hole-in-the-Wall Stew, Corn Fritters, Roast Deer and Venison, Sourdough Cornbread, Red Chili Biscuits and Potato Pancakes.

More restaurants and food services in *The Territory* are described under the other towns and villages. In Tincup: *The Grubstake Hash House* and the *Golden Nugget Miner's Bar*. In Diablo: the *El Paso Del Norte Cafe*, *Lost Donkey Cantina* and the *Market Plaza Wagons*. In Jackrabbit Flats: the *Crippled Dog Saloon*. At Fort Carson: the *Post Bakery* and the *Post Kitchen & Mess Hall*. At the Broken Spur Ranch: *The Cook's Shack*, and at the Cordova Hacienda: a *Ranch House Breakfast*.

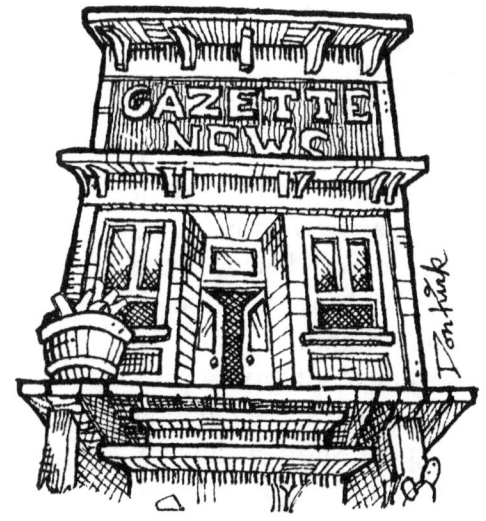

WORKING CRAFTS AND RETAIL SHOPS
at Wagon Wheel Gap

"A push-the-button-to-make-it-happen mentality is replacing the joy and sense of self-worth derived from expended effort. What's important now is the 'done' and not the 'doing'."
— Donald Wright, *Model Railroader*

WORKING CRAFT EXHIBITS. These businesses demonstrate nineteenth-century crafts and sell their hand-made wares. The craftsmen actually work on their products as guests look on. Guests are invited to ask questions about the process. Some of the craftspeople who work these exhibits are retired and live in the resort villages of the park. There are also programs available where the younger generation can learn the almost lost "Old World" crafts, to preserve them for future generations. The list below covers only those crafts found in the main town of *Wagon Wheel Gap*. Others will be described under the other villages in **The Territory** and include such things as quilting, chair caining, making cord wool, weaving, soap making, leather work, rug hooking, tin smithing, etc.

The **WAGON WHEEL GAZETTE Newspaper Office**. Newspapers were vital to the economy of a small town. Advertisements for land and business opportunities filled the newsprint, and articles by *Horace Greeley* brought many men West with his call "Go West, young man". This news office is completely furnished with period antiques and uses an original operating moveable type, flat-bed printing press to produce paper products for *The Territory*: the *Wagon Wheel Gazette* **newspaper** where guests can read about the exploits of famous outlaws and lawmen and events at the resort, **outlaw wanted posters**, **reproduction dime novels**, **advertising brochures**, **broadsides** and **gift items** like the "Code of the West" poster. At the news office, guests can see how the **printing process** was accomplished in the nineteenth century: hand-set type was laid into "chases" by the typesetters, the press inked, and each page pressed sheet by sheet. The newspaper office also has a photo section that pays tribute to **the journalists** who first chronicled the West and were instrumental in

drawing settlers to the West: famous writers like *Robert Louis Stevenson, William Sydney Porter* (O. Henry), *Samuel Bowles* and *Samuel Clemens* (Mark Twain). There are also examples of the woodcut illustrator's art on display.

HORACE PUTNEY PHOTOGRAPHY (Museum and Portrait Studio). Photography was a novelty in the mid 1800's and cowboys lined up to get their photos taken in duded-up outfits. They would send these overstated photos back to their families in the East. With a collection of Western and Victorian outfits, individuals and families can be photographed with a view camera to produce old-fashioned tintypes. Girls can dress as saloon girls or southern belles, men can "play" the Civil War soldier, town marshal or gunfighter. This type of retail shop is already popular around the country, but this one will try to be different by recreating the photo studio just as it would have looked in the early days of photography, with hand-painted backdrops and antique props. The studio also serves as a museum displaying actual **antique cameras and equipment** and has demonstrations of **photoprocessing techniques** of the period: *tintypes* and *daguerreotypes*, wet-plate negative developing, the use of flashpowder, etc. A tribute is made to **the photographers** that first recorded the West on film such as *Joseph Smith* and *Mathew Brady*. Guests can also purchase film here for their own picture taking in ***The Territory***. The best "picture points", with the best time of day, are listed in a free brochure and the photographer will give the guests pointers to taking good pictures in the park.

TINY FLINN'S BLACKSMITH SHOP. A hefty, leather-skinned smithy can be seen practicing his trade, pounding out red-hot iron over a flaming furnace. The blacksmith makes tires for wagon wheels, hinges for cattle gates, hardware for wagons, and shoes for horses. He sharpens plows, repairs farm machinery and in his spare time designs and constructs **iron puzzles** to amuse travelers. These and other IRONWORK GIFTS are available for sale.

BIRD'S BOOT & SADDLE SHOP. Here guests can see a bootmaker construct nineteenth-century FOOTWEAR exactly the way it was done over 100 years ago. Available for sale are historically correct "straight-last" brogans, knee-high cavalry boots and cowboy boots made in the original styling and tradition of the Old West. All are hand stitched with wooden pegs and square iron nails. Guests can be fitted for custom orders, or purchase standard sizes on display in the shop. Ladies period shoes and lace-up boots are stocked as well as LEATHER GOODS like holsters and spur straps.

WHEELRIGHT, JESSE MORALES, PROPRIETOR. Step onto a floor of sawdust and wood chips and into a large room with shuttered

windows that open up to the outdoors. Here guests can see the construction of wagon wheels, barrels, and furniture that will be used in *The Territory*. This almost lost craft will be there to view and guests can ask questions of the craftsmen. Guests will also see a collection of original HAND-CARVED DOLLS AND TOYS (Reproductions based on originals copied from museum pieces are available at gift shops in *The Territory*).

SARA-JENE'S CANDLE SHOP. We don't think about artificial light today—it's everywhere at the flip of a switch—but it was the end of the eighteenth century before there were any advancements in lighting technology. Before that, candles were the only way to light up the night's darkness. And it wasn't until the nineteenth century that candles where made of paraffin instead of the low-melting-point animal tallow or beeswax. *Sadie* will tell the kids all about the safe use of candles and show them the fascinating art of CANDLEMAKING using techniques that are centuries old. Decorative candles, molds, holders, tin lanterns, oil lamps—all manner of early lighting instruments are on display, and are for sale.

HENDERSON LUMBER & FENCING is an actual working late-nineteenth-century sawmill built to supply rough-sawn timbers and board lumber for building the towns and structures in *The Territory*. One of the buildings displays the tools used by **carpenters, millwrights and coopers** and includes models, dioramas, photographs and paintings showing the life and times of the lumbermen. Most of the towns of the West were initially built of wood, a durable, stable material. Trees were chopped down and sawed into planks:

> Lumbermen and sawmill operators were in great demand: skills that built the West . . . The search for lumber, the felling of trees, the milling, the utilization, the building of bunkhouses and mess halls, the erection of lumber yards, the drying of lumber—all of the processes that went into the utilization of this most valuable material contributed much to the building of the West.
> — David R. Phillips, *The West: An American Experience*

DUEY'S ICE PLANT is an experimental contraption of mechanical genius designed to produce ice for *Wagon Wheel Gap*. It's a marvel of engineering by an inventor who has immigrated from France. It still has a few "bugs" to be worked out, but *Gabriel Duey* is selling ice to the restaurants and saloons in *The Territory*. Visitors to *W.W.G.* can now get ice for their drinks!

RETAIL SHOPS
ON NEXT PAGE

The gift shops in *RedRock Canyon Territory* cater to the western buff (and those who want to give a gift to their favorite western fan) with a comprehensive collection of products: books, music, videotapes, clothing, memorabilia, souvenirs, and accoutrements for living history fans.

HENLEY BOOKS sells BOOKS relating to the Old West and Western movies: outlaws and lawmen, Indians, pioneers, railroading, guns, buckskinning, military history, crafts, etc. A complete collection of paperbacks from *Max Brand, Zane Grey* and *Louis L'Amour* can be found here along with a display of memorabilia honoring these great western writers. Also available are VIDEOTAPES and LASERDISCS of Westerns. The shop sits next to the *Badlands Movie House*.

MUSIC SHOP. Original 19th-century MUSICAL INSTRUMENTS are on display here. Guests can purchase reproduction instruments (*guitars, banjos, concertinas, harmonicas, juice harps, drums, flutes,* etc.), sheet music, tapes and audio CD's. Period music is played on a speaker system in the store. **Movie soundtracks** can also be purchased here. The shop sits adjacent to the *Badlands Movie House*.

H. B. FRANK DRYGOODS stocks a complete collection of authentic reproduction CIVILIAN PERIOD CLOTHING and accessories for living history buffs and re-enactors. Men can buy Old West frock coats, buckskin jackets, shirts, trousers, vests and neckties. Ladies are well represented with day dresses, ballgowns, period undergarments, parasols, feather fans, etc. There is also a collection of children's period clothing, patterns, bolts of cloth, buttons, etc. Available too, are coach bags, boot spurs, marshal's badges, pocket watches, bandannas, suspenders, etc.

HENNESSEY'S HABERDASHERY has a large selection of western-era HATS. From "five-gallon" Stetsons to English bowler hats. Hats for the rugged working cowboy to the finely dressed Victorian gentleman. Also available are accessories like neckties, handkerchiefs, gloves, pocket watches, walking canes, etc.

ARTHUR OVERSTREET'S CIGAR STORE has pipes, tobacco, cigars and other sundries for the successful businessman in *Wagon Wheel Gap*.

EXISTING MUSEUMS FOR STUDY:
Nevada City Museum, Nevada City, Montana.
South Park City Museum, Fairplay, Colorado.
Panhandle Plains Historic Museum, Canyon, Texas.
Lumberman's Museum, Patton, Massachusetts.
British Columbia Forest Museum, B.C., Canada.

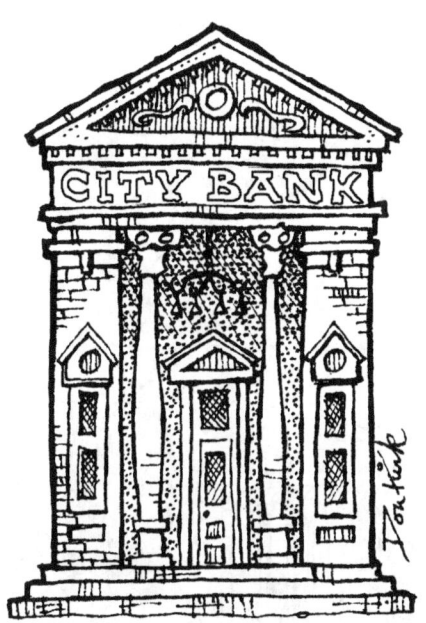

INFORMATION AND ASSISTANCE
at Wagon Wheel Gap

"If the Sentinel is a little thin this morning, just bear in mind that the telegraph office was moving yesterday, the mail from the East didn't come in and there wasn't anybody in town who had enough accommodation to die, get married or have a baby."
— *The Daily Sentinel*, Laramie, Wyoming, 1875

Behind the Victorian false-fronts of the Old West towns are the facilities and services needed by the guests of the twentieth century. The services are clearly marked on the territorial maps handed out to guests.

The **TERRITORIAL MARSHAL'S OFFICE** is the COMMUNICATIONS HEADQUARTERS of *The Territory*. For the public, it provides information, security personnel, lost & found, and first aid.

The **TELEGRAPH OFFICE** can be found at the main railroad depot and provides actual old-time telegraph communication to the other villages in *The Territory*. For communication outside the park, modern TELEPHONE SERVICE and Western Union TELEGRAMS are available. Any information related to park activities and accommodations is also available at each depot.

The **PONY EXPRESS OFFICE** is the official POST OFFICE of the park. It has outgoing mail services, postage stamps, postcards, stationery and envelopes. All mail is taken out of *The Territory* by *Pony Express* riders. The mail is canceled with a special "Pony Express" stamp. Arriving mail is announced by hoisting a flag out front.

CLARENCE TUTTLE'S CITY BANK provides the following BANKING SERVICES: credit card advances, traveler's checks cashed, and *Opera House* and special events tickets can be purchased. U. S. currency can be converted to *Frontier Money* printed by the bank for use at many businesses in *The Territory* (see "Park Entrance" for an explanation of *Frontier Money*.)

NEWSPAPER OFFICE IN BUCKSKIN JOE, COLORADO

UNDERTAKER'S SHOP IN BUCKSKIN JOE

PART III: THE VILLAGES

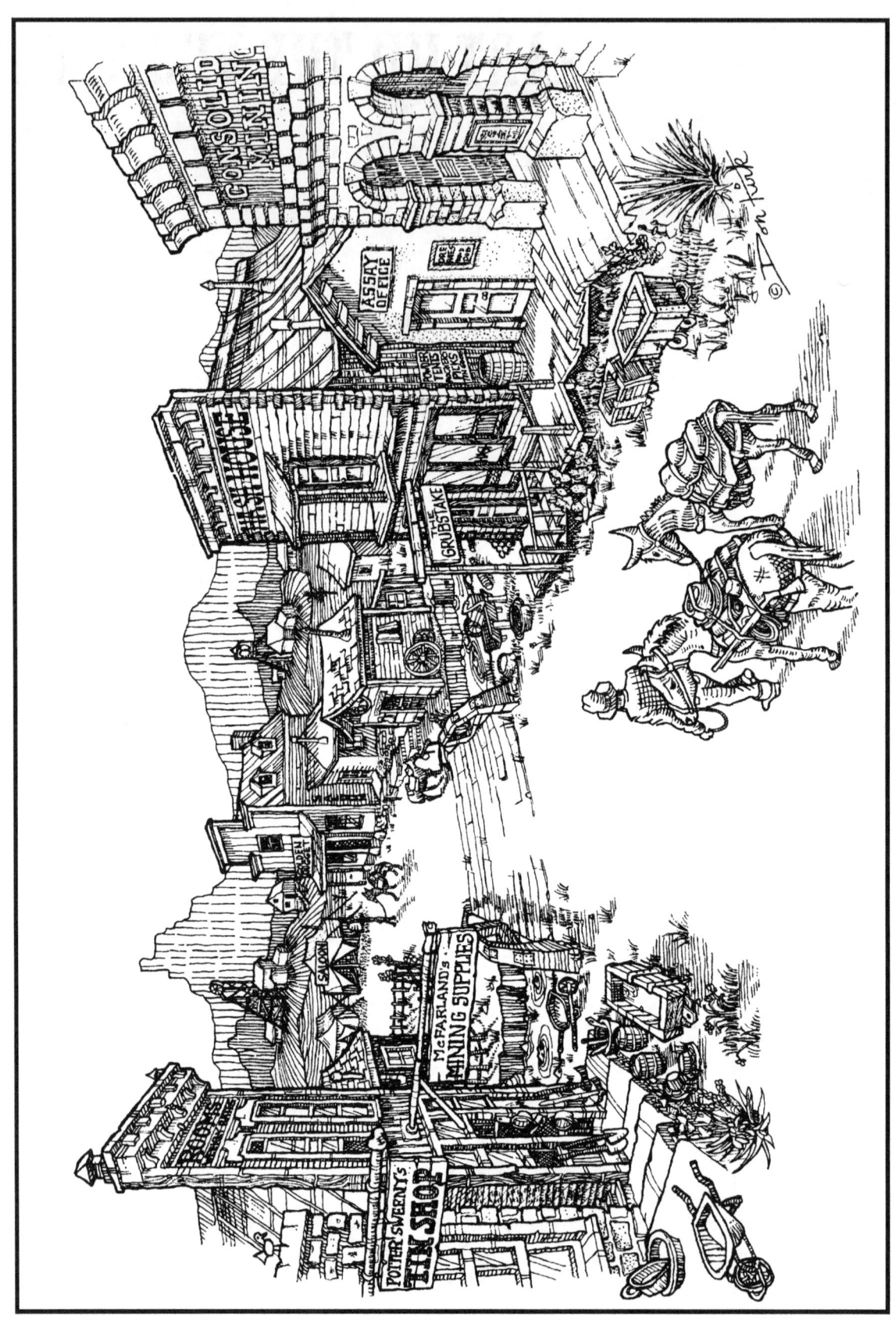

VIEW OF TINCUP IN DEAD HORSE CANYON

PART III-2 REDROCK CANYON TERRITORY © DON KIRK

DEAD HORSE CANYON
MINING DISTRICT

The Town Of TINCUP
And The MURDOCK GOLD & SILVER MINING & MILLING CO.

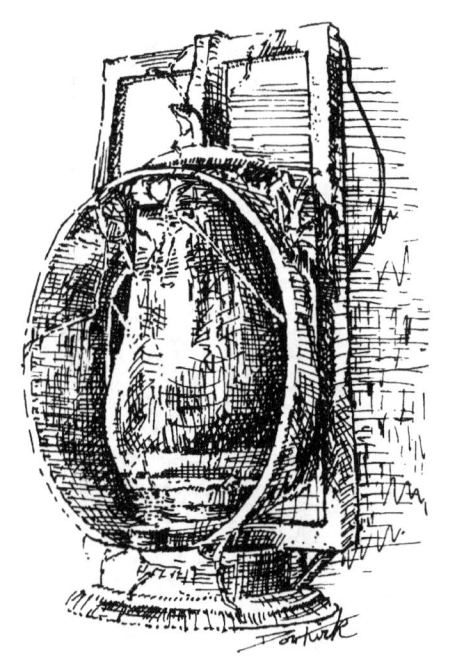

"The growth of western mining camps reflects the frontier struggle of man to build something lasting in a strange and frequently hostile environment. It becomes a story of the men and women who lived and died there, who called it home."

— Duane A. Smith, *Rocky Mountain Mining Camps*

A prospector that went by the name of "Washtub Willie" stooped by a mountain stream and dipped out a drink of water with his tin cup. Mixed with the cool water were flakes of sparkling gold . . . and so began the town of *Tincup*. A placer and hard rock **mining camp**, *Tincup* consists of a small cluster of large canvas tents with wooden floors and side-walls of pine; boardwalks over muddy streets and the beginnings of more permanent "balloon-frame" structures as the town grows in population and riches. Smoke rises from the chimneys. It is populated by hard-working miners, gamblers, swindlers and ladies of the evening. It's a tough town with its own miner's laws, and a wild, boisterous life style. It's a hard drinking, gambling, bawdy, rough-and-ready town, not yet civilized with the family institutions of education, religion and culture. Guests will find donkeys roaming free in the streets, and miners fighting in the mud. The town is situated, rough-shod and rambling, along *Fool's Creek* in *Dead Horse Canyon*. The canyon is surrounded by hills spotted with mining claims. The rich *Murdock Gold & Silver Mining and Milling Company* sits high on a hill overlooking the camp.

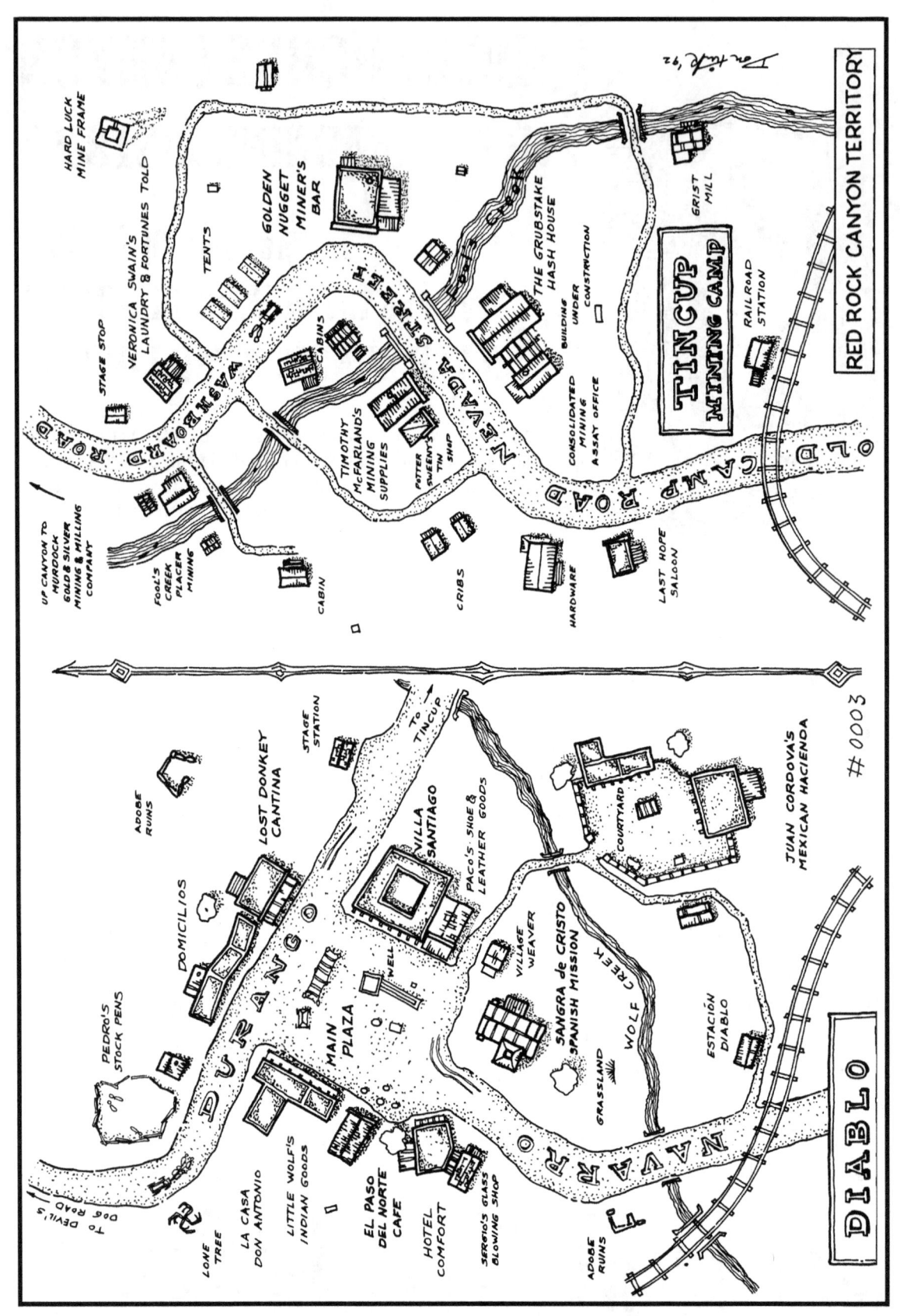

MAP OF DIABLO AND TINCUP

THE TOWN OF TINCUP

The "businesses" in *Tincup* include the following places to explore (see map # 0003, page III-4):

(exhibit)   **TIMOTHY McFARLAND'S MINING SUPPLIES** is a "practical set" completely furnished with reproductions of period tools and provisions: picks, shovels, sledge hammers, kegs of blasting powder, rockers, tents, canvas overalls, canned goods, tinware, etc. Everything a miner needs to practice his trade. Related gift items are for sale.

(exhibit)   **CONSOLIDATED MINING ASSAY OFFICE** is a small recreated *practical set* with its scales and steel safe. It also has a room with a photo history of gold and silver mining in the United States, from the California 49ers to the '97 Klondike discoveries.

(entment)   **VERONICA SWAIN'S LAUNDRY & FORTUNES TOLD** is a wooden-floored canvas tent with an attached wooden shack where guests can actually get their fortunes told and maybe some clothes washed.

(gifts)   **POTTER SWEENY'S TIN SHOP** is a retail shop containing graniteware, Mexican pottery, tinware and other gift items.

(drinks)   **THE GOLDEN NUGGET MINER'S BAR** is the place to go after a hard day in the mines. Guests can wash down that mine dust with the explosive *Red Dynamite, Blue Ruin, Irish Whiskey* or the 76er's favorite *Forty Rod* which will fell a man at that distance even around a corner. These are unique, tasty non-alcoholic drinks for the entire family. MINER'S COURT (live entertainment) is usually held at *The Golden Nugget* and is presided over by *Harry O'Flannagan*. The miners—far away from their homes in the East, without any influence from Eastern law—had to dispense their own justice based on the laws decided on by the miners. Here guests can see a realistic reenactment of a miner's court performed by the *Sourdough Mining Company Players* with guests participating as the jury.

(food)   **THE GRUBSTAKE HASH HOUSE** is the place to go for some good old-fashioned "miner's grub" that might include "son-of-a-gun" stew, sourdough biscuits and hot peach cobbler. In a dimly-lit room filled with tables made of clapboard siding, there is much joviality as a musician tickles the keys of a dark mahogany upright

REDROCK CANYON TERRITORY © DON KIRK

piano and a second player strums a banjo and blows through a harmonica clinched in his teeth. It's a routy, rambunctious place of fun. Full meals are served here.

(entment) **SOURDOUGH MINING COMPANY PLAYERS.** STREET ENTERTAINMENT is always taking place in the streets of *Tincup*. Guests might see miners fighting in the mud over the only woman in town, a prospector wandering through town dragging with him his trusty mule loaded with tools and provisions, or a placer miner riding into town screaming "Eurika" at the top of his lungs because he has just found the Mother Lode!

(trail) **MINING CLAIMS** marked by HEADFRAMES and mine tailings dot the hills around *Tincup*. Hard-won mines with names like the *Hard Luck, Independence, Last Hope, Golden Queen, Cash & Luck,* and *Sourdough*. These mines provide a backdrop for the town of *Tincup* and provide places to explore by mule or on foot.

(entment) **FOOL'S CREEK PLACER MINING.** In a *salted* creek, guests can actually play prospector and pan for *color*. Guests learn the "tricks" to successful panning the way the prospectors do it: how to select the right spot and how to "wash out" a pan and use a *cradle*. *Fool's Creek* was so named not because it was foolish to try to find gold in it, but because the creek runs in a direction which appears to be contrary to the natural drainage. The diagonal strata of the canyon walls aiding in the illusion.

(exhibits) **OTHER BUILDINGS** in *Tincup* include the *Last Hope Saloon*, **brothel cribs, tent residents** and several **miner's cabins**.

REDROCK CANYON TERRITORY © DON KIRK

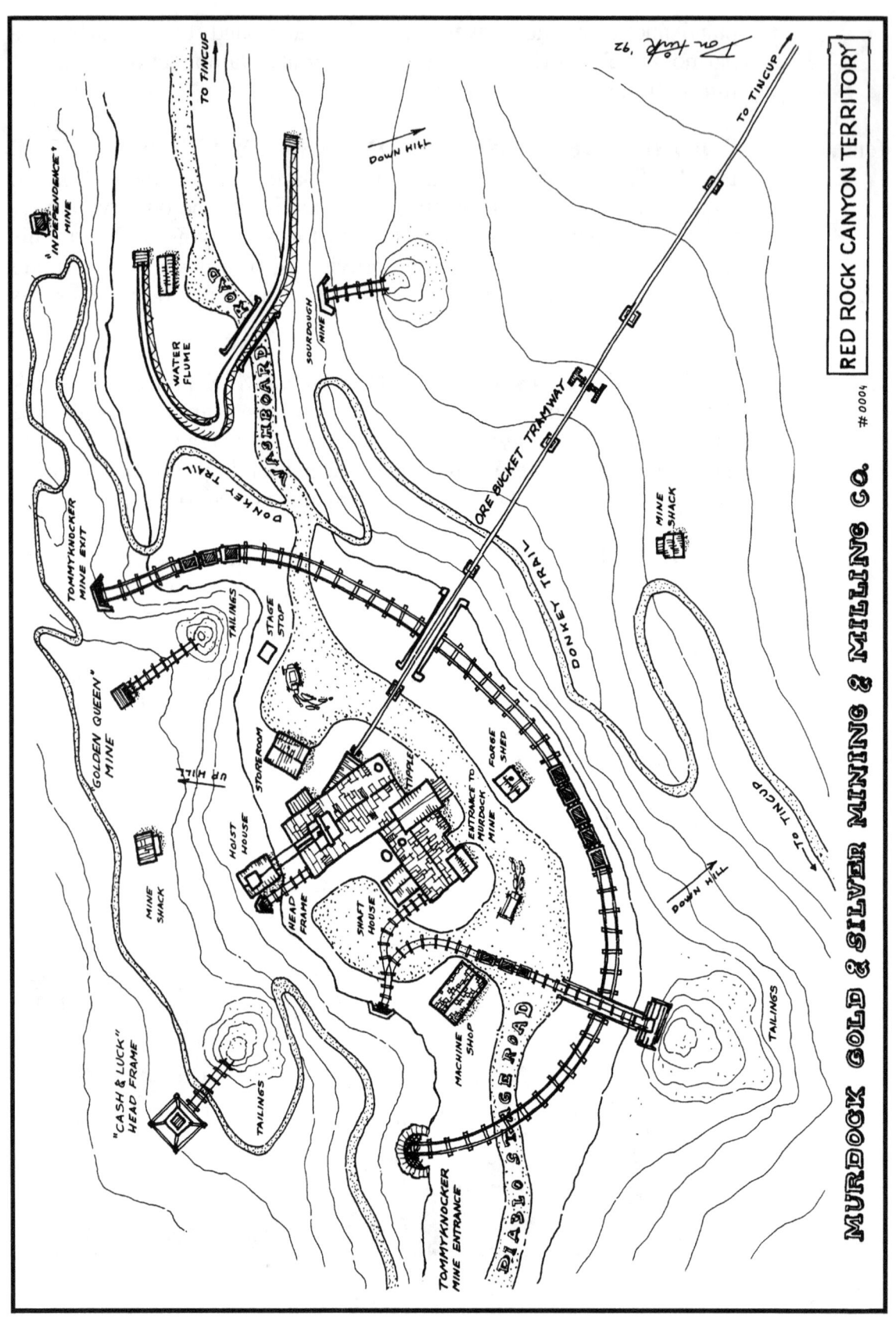

MAP OF MURDOCK GOLD & SILVER MINING & MILLING CO.

PART III-8   REDROCK CANYON TERRITORY © DON KIRK

MURDOCK GOLD & SILVER MINING & MILLING CO.

This mining operation, actually three rides and a museum, sits high on *Bald Eagle Mountain*, overlooking the mining camp. An aerial *Ore-Bucket Tram* brings guests up to the mine from *Tincup*. Guests can also take the stage up the winding *Gold Hill Road* to the mining complex. The *Murdock Gold & Silver Mining & Milling Company* is a scaled-down reproduction of a gold mine in the Old West. It's made up of a number of buildings, all arranged and tied together to be pleasing to the movie camera as viewed from the mining town below, and at "picture points" ABOVE the mine that reveal both mine, town and valley beyond. Above ground guests can see the **shaft house, head frame, hoist house, lift house, tipple, machine shop** and **storeroom**. Below ground is a series of tunnels and caverns "shored up" with large wood timbers (see map # 0004, page III-8).

(ride)   The **ORE-BUCKET TRAM** originates in *Tincup* and like an aerial skyway, takes passengers up a steep incline on a cable system. The design is fashioned after actual aerial trams used to haul raw iron ore out of the mines and over to the processing mills. Passengers can ride the tram in both directions or take a stage for the return trip.

(museum)   The **MURDOCK MINING MUSEUM** allows guests to WALK through the mining complex, through doors, up stairs and through winding tunnels to explore the inner workings of a gold mining operation. Guests learn about tunneling, shoring, ventilation, pumping water, and the processing of minerals.

(ride) The **TOMMYKNOCKER MINE RIDE** takes the guest around the mining complex, through buildings, down air shafts, and through solid rock tunnels. It's an exciting and educational trip by "ore car" on tracks through the mine complex and through the underground tunnels and shafts. Listen to the dripping of water and the echo of men working deep in the mine. The ore cars drop down a vertical shaft on a thrilling journey as the cars jump and shutter through cave-ins, falling timbers, broken trackage, "dust" clouds, underground streams, mine leprechauns (called "tommyknockers") and other dangers that lurk at every turn. Travel deep into a mountain of fun, mystery and adventure.

The ride ends as you find the glowing vein of the Mother Lode. (The ride is not actually underground, but is built in a building placed on the side of the hill hidden from view. Different from a roller coaster ride, cars move much slower and change directions horizontally and vertically.)

(exhibit) The **DEAD HORSE CANYON WATER FLUME** is a wooden water flume that winds down the rugged hillside past water wheels and *sluice boxes*. Water was the miner's most valuable tool and when gold had "played out" in the streams, more elaborate techniques were required to get at the gold. Hard rock mining resulted, and water was required to wash away the top soil. Water flumes were built to carry water across mountains and valleys to the mining site. For sport, adventurous soles would attempt to "ride" the flumes, and in those days, they did it without a vessel to ride in! This wooden re-creation is built to look like the originals and demonstrates their function.

(ride) The **TINCUP TRAIN DEPOT** is a tiny one room station where guests can take the train to the next town down the line.

(ride) The **GOLDFIELD OVERLAND EXPRESS STAGE STATION** gives guests and opportunity to get out of town fast. The stage makes stops at all towns and villages in *The Territory*.

Most of today's existing ghost towns of the American West were often short-lived mining boom towns that had a major influence on the settlement of the West. Because of their location, usually high in the mountains, they developed a unique character that makes them visually distinctive from other kinds of frontier towns, so to preserve that character, the *Dead Horse Canyon Mining District* is also uniquely different from the rest of the towns in *RedRock Canyon Territory*.

EXISTING MINES FOR STUDY:

Victor Mining District, Cripple Creek, AZ
Vulture Gold Mine, Wickenburg, AZ
Mollie Kathleen Gold Mine, Cripple Creek, CO
The Queen Copper Mine, Bisbee, AZ
Argo Gold Mill, Idaho Springs, CO
Hundred Gold Mine, Silverton, CO
Bachelor-Syracuse Mine, Ouray, CO
Blue Bell Mine, Eurika, Utah.
Maude Munroe Mine, Idaho Springs, CO
The Standard Mill, Bodie, CA
Sunnyside Mine and Mill, Silverton, CO
Edgar Mine, Idaho Springs, CO

MINING MUSEUMS FOR STUDY:

Tonapah Mining Museum, Tonapah, NV
District Mining Museum, Cripple Creek, CO
Robson's Arizona Mining World, Aguila, AZ
Old Coal Mine Museum, Madrid, NM
Arizona Mining and Mineral Museum, Phoenix, AZ
Jerome State Historic Park, Jerome, AZ
New Mexico Museum of Mining, Grants, NM
Western Museum of Mining and Industry, Colorado Springs, CO
Ore-Bucklet Tramway, Pioche, NV.

The Town of DIABLO
A Mexican Village

30 Miles To Water
20 Miles To Wood
10 Inches To Hell
Gone Back East To Wife's Family.
  — sign on door of abandoned shack,
      Texas Panhandle, 1910

Diablo is a small Mexican village that sits alone on the dry and barren *Dagger Flats* where only cacti and gila monsters reign. The town of *Diablo* is an oasis on the desert: a natural spring bubbling from the rocks allows the growth of a few trees that provide cool welcome shade to travelers. The village is a quiet, relaxed place except when people arrive for parties and weddings. It's a place both for **siestas** AND **fiestas**. It's a place for weddings, parties, eating and sleeping. Much of the town is built of stuccoed adobe sun-dried bricks, with timber and mud roofs, and dirt and flagstone floors. The white-washed stucco is accented with bright color from pastel trimwork, flags, Mexican blankets, lanterns and *piñatas*. A number of buildings, with patios and verandahs, surround a main market plaza. A water fountain and washing area sits in the middle of the plaza and is surrounded by tables and benches on cobblestones. The streets of *Navarro* and *Durango* radiate out from the plaza (see map # 0003, page III-4).

(exhibit)   **SANGRA de CRISTO SPANISH MISSION** at one end of town is a *practical set* completely furnished with pews and an alter. It is an ideal setting for **weddings** and religious special events with guests costumed in period garb. After the wedding, the reception can take place in the plaza and the bride and groom can spend the night at *Cordova's Hacienda*.

(drink) The **LOST DONKEY CANTINA** in *Diablo* serves unique **soft drinks** patterned after the beers and liquors of the Old West like the *Tequila Twister, Taos Lighting* and *Apache Cactus Beer*. The cantina is in a dimly lit room with a bar made by laying wood planks over whiskey barrels. Lit only by lanterns, the cantina is a haunting "watering hole" with peeling plaster, cobwebs and banditos lurking in the shadows. A shootout can be expected at any time.

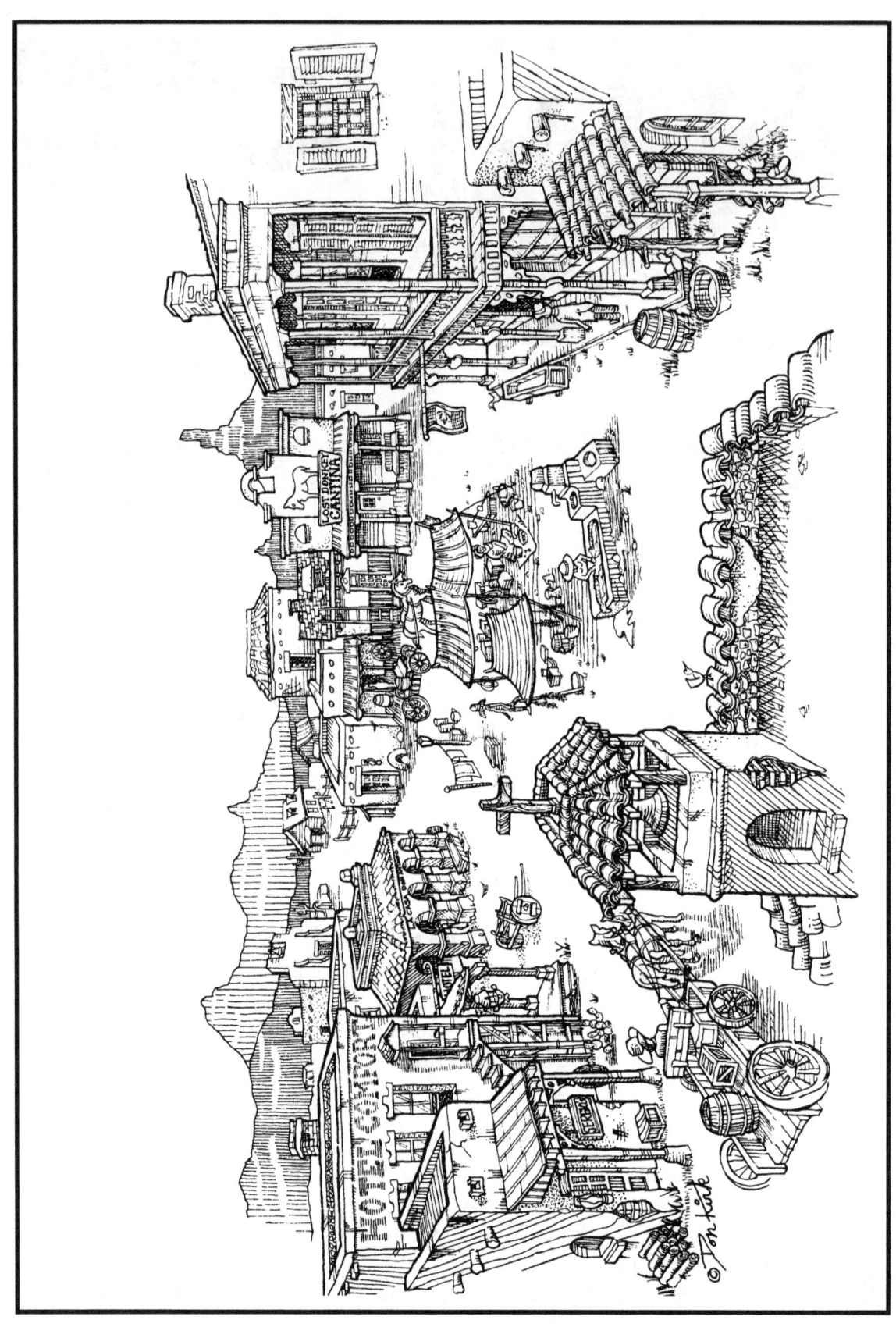

DIABLO'S MAIN PLAZA

(food)   The **El PASO DEL NORTE CAFE** serves authentic "Texas Borderland" food in a quiet, secluded atmosphere; a setting designed to work as a *practical set*. The menu includes red-hot chili, green enchiladas, sizzling fajitas, beef tacos al carbon, jalapeno pineapple coleslaw, and frozen mango dessert. The meal can be washed down with margaritas or white sangria. A **Mexican breakfast** is served here at sunrise for those early riser photographers and guests. Try huevos rancheros, pecan flapjacks, or pistachio sticky buns!

(food &) During the day, the **MAIN PLAZA** is an open-air market where **food**, wares and gifts can be bought from canopied lean-tos and two-wheeled carts: juice drinks squeezed from fresh fruit, Mexican candies and pastries, sopapillas with honey, charros rolled in cinnamon and sugar, ice-cream, hot chili and grilled corn on the cob. Hand-crafted toys from Mexico are also sold. In the plaza you'll find all kinds of **entertaining** "characters" hawking their goods. Guests will see spinners, weavers and potters at work. At night, just as it happened in the Old West, the plaza becomes an open-air restaurant with wooden tables scattered across the plaza. There is "Fandango" music and dancing in a plaza lit only by lantern light and the rays of light from open doorways.

(ride)   **PEDRO'S STOCK PENS**, just outside of town, provide **mule and burro rides** into the surrounding bush. Fun for all ages, short trips are made on mule or mule-pulled cart into the prairie, around cacti and adobe ruins of all kinds.

(sleep)   **JUAN CORDOVA'S MEXICAN HACIENDA** is situated just outside of Diablo. It has a two-story main house, a courtyard surrounded by a low adobe wall and several outbuildings all with an authentic "south-of-the-border" flavor. The hacienda is designed for overnight accommodations and breakfast services much like a "Bed-and-Breakfast Inn".

(exhibit) **HOTEL COMFORT** is a small two story "south of the border" hotel used as a *practical set* and it's open for guests to explore. It's furnished with hand-carved beds, dressers and chairs. Plaster is peeling off the adobe walls, the bed spreads, tattered. It can be used for interior film shooting.

(museum) **VILLA SANTIAGO** is a *practical set* and museum of a typical home of a well-to-do Spanish colonial family. Living and servant's quarters are completely furnished with early 1800's furniture. Original paintings hang on the walls. The exterior walls of this fortress-like home are made of four-foot-thick adobe and inside are

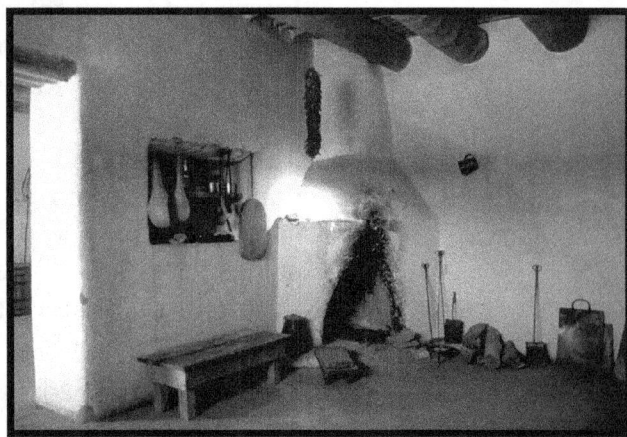

REDROCK CANYON TERRITORY © DON KIRK

hand-hewn *vigas* to support the roof. The small white-washed rooms surround an open courtyard.

(craft) **SERGIO'S GLASS BLOWING SHOP** makes glass vases, stained glass, knickknacks, etc. and *Sergio* demonstrates the process of glass blowing, casting, and coldworking procedures. His works of glass art are for sale.

(craft) At **PACO'S SHOE & LEATHER GOODS,** guests can watch *Paco* make, by hand, many kinds of authentic reproductions of leather goods found in the nineteenth century: gunbelts, holsters, spur leathers, horse tack, moccasins, sandals, chaps, jackets, etc.

(craft) The **VILLAGE WEAVER** can be seen making all kinds of hand-woven goods: baskets, tapestries, blankets, etc. An old loom and early weaving tools are put to use for the guests to see the process.

(gift) **LITTLE WOLF'S INDIAN GOODS** is where you can find authentically hand-crafted Native-American goods like pottery, blankets, cloth, jewelry, beads, etc.

(gift) **LA CASA DON ANTONIO**. Here guests will find for sale fine Mexican, Guatemalan and southwestern handcrafts. Porcelain china, painted tiles, clothing, ceramics, stoneware, crystal, sculpture and folk art. Only items that would have existed in the eighteenth and nineteenth century are sold here.

(ride) The **ESTACION DIABLO** is a tiny "whistle stop" that allows guests to take the train to the other towns in *The Territory*.

(ride) The **SWEETWATER EXPRESS STAGE STATION** is another place you can go to get a ride on a stage to the next town.

EXISTING MISSIONS FOR STUDY:
Mission San Carlos Borromeo, Carmel, Calif.
San Juan Bautista S.H.S., San Juan Bautista, Calif.
La Pudrisima Mission S.H.S., Lompoc, Calif.
Chapel of San Miguel, Santa Fe, New Mexico.
Mission San Juan Capistrano, San Antonio, Texas.
San Xavier del Bac, Tucson, Arizona.
SOME HOMES:
Spanish Governor's Palace, San Antonio, Texas.
La Casa Magoffin, El Paso, Texas.
Martinez Hacienda, Taos, New Mexico.
Kit Carson Home, Taos, New Mexico.
Baca House, Trinidad, Colorado.
Old Cienega Village Museum, Santa Fe, New Mexico.

THE ONLY STREET IN JACKRABBIT FLATS

JACKRABBIT FLATS
A Ghost Town

"If nothing else, a ghost town will give you respect for the tenacity of man and the power of nature. That any living being, much less communities numbering in the thousands, could survive and prosper in these desolate, parched wastelands is a wonder."
— Yvette Cardozo, *Ghost Riders*, Camping Journal

Jackrabbit Flats is a wind-swept Ghost Town that has seen better days. It once was a town with a dream. Now it's abandoned and dilapidated; canted buildings with sway-backed roofs and falling porches. Faded business signs swing in the breeze. Rickety boardwalks, sun and rain-worn siding barely clings on to life. Guests can peek into the dusty windows and see cobweb-covered furniture and playing cards still sitting on poker tables. Guests here the saloon doors and windmill creaking in the dry wind and see the tumbleweeds as they scurry by to take a peek at the out-of-town strangers.

(ride)   **TRAIN DEPOT:** When the train pulls up to this podunk station with its elevation sign blowing in the breeze and the only sound on the wind is that of a squeaking windmill, you'll wonder why you decided to disembark at this whistle stop. But take a walk into town and see what it has to offer.

(drink)   **CRIPPLED DOG SALOON:** Guests can enter through the swinging doors of the only saloon in town. Inside guests will find that there is still a living barkeep behind the bar ready to serve them. You might also see a couple of other travelers at a corner table. Someone may even tinkle a tune at the upright piano.

(exhibit)   **SHERIFF'S OFFICE & JAIL:** Step into *Sheriff Munson Taylor's* office and see if there are still any outlaws in the cool dark cells in the back. Guests will find the skeletal remains of a badman who was left behind. Glance at the old, faded wanted posters of famous outlaws. Note the coffee pot still sitting on the pot-bellied stove, now covered with a few cobwebs.

REDROCK CANYON TERRITORY © DON KIRK   PART III-17

(entment) **PROVISIONS & DRYGOODS:** The store is now boarded up and abandoned, but guests can peek through the windows and see ghostly cowboys playing checkers by the pot-bellied stove. The storekeep is seen selling cloth to a semi-transparent customer! Mirrored projection effects do the trick.

(exhibit) **BOOT HILL CEMETERY** sits just outside of town on a hill overlooking the wind-swept town. Ornate wrought-iron fencing enclose elaborate markers. Tall, slender monuments of wood sit askew—a lone name chiseled into the weathered wood. A tall ornate marble obelisk marks the grave of the cattle baron that once built the town. Heavy-hearted thoughts go to the people who tried hard to settle the area and make a living here. Be careful where you step, you might find an open grave; and why are there fresh flowers on one of the headstones?

(entment) **NIGHT LIFE.** In the evenings, you'll hear wolves howling in the distance and the sound of a player piano coming from nowhere in particular!

(ride) **STAGE STOP:** Guests can leave town by way of the *Sweetwater Overland Express* stage or any *Freighter* that might pass through town. But you can't be in hurry, the stage doesn't always live up to its name.

Boothill Cemetery, Virginia City, Nevada

Below is a sampling of historic towns, most of which began as mining towns, some of which never developed beyond the first stage as log buildings before going broke, others progressed to wooden balloon framing with the use of the sawmill, and still others survived catastorphic fires and buildings were rebuilt in brick. Some are pure ghost towns, secluded from modern civilization with not a single soul living there. Some are protected by private or state ownership and others have become boom towns again!

EXISTING "GHOST TOWNS" FOR STUDY:

Bodie, near Bridgeport, California	State Historic Site
Nevada City, near Virginia City, MT	Museum
Barkerville, British Columbia, Canada	Historic site
Calico, California	State Historic Site
Elkhorn, Montana	Ghost Town
St. Elmo, Colorado	Semi-Ghost Town
Knott's Berry Farm, California	Theme park
Fayette State Park, Garden, Michigan	Historical site
Columbia, Sonora, California	State Historic Park
Bannack, Dillon, Montana	State Park
Garnet, Montana	State Park
Rawhide, Scottsdale, Arizona	Re-creation
Silver Plume, Colorado	Ex-Ghost Town
Silver City, Idaho	Semi-ghost
Goldpoint, Nevada	Semi-ghost
Shakespeare, New Mexico	Ghost Town
Madrid, New Mexico	Tourist Town
Grafton, Utah	Ghost Town
Trail Town, Cody, Wyoming	Re-creation
Lincoln, New Mexico	Living Town
Ashcroft, Colorado	Semi-ghost
Berlin-Ichthyosaur, Nevada	State Park
South Pass City, Wyoming	State Park

Silver Plume, Colorado

THE QUADRANGLE AT FORT CARSON

FORT CARSON
A Frontier Outpost

"The labors, endurance, and combats of the western [cavalry soldier] created the framework of law and order that made settlement and social development possible . . . We need to know more about our military past and the men who loved it, just as we need to deepen our understanding of all facets of the American experience."
— Don Rickey, Jr., *Forty Miles A Day On Beans And Hay*, 1963

FORTS WERE ESTABLISHED early in the West to foster trade with the Indians and with Mexico. Later they were used as waystations for pioneers trekking west and as relay points for the stage lines and the short-lived *Pony Express*. Eventually, many became cavalry garrisons to protect settlers and fight the Indians. Forts were an oasis in a wild, wide open land where settlers, mountain men, traders and Indians could trade goods and draw provisions for their return trip back into wilderness territory.

Butted up against rugged rock outcroppings, *Fort Carson* is a compound of several "scaled-down" buildings surrounding a small parade ground. The compound is enclosed by a stockade built of adobe and logs. The buildings are constructed of weathered adobe, stone, limestone block and large timbers. A large double-doored gate opens into the fort. The fort is aesthetically designed for camera views from any angle and some of the buildings contain "practical" interiors.

(info)   **THE POST HEADQUARTERS** is where you can find **information** about living history events and trail rides into the hills. The staff is dressed in the clothing of the period representing fur trappers, Indian scouts, settlers, and Cavalry troopers. There are scheduled living history lectures on historical subjects relating to frontier outposts: Indian fighting, fur trading, post life, woman in the

West, and the comparing of myth with the historic reality. There are **horseback trail rides** into the surrounding hills and prairie.

(museum) **THE POST WAREHOUSE** is a **cavalry museum** containing a display of authentic Civil War and Indian War uniforms, accoutrements, weapons, photographs, battle flags, horse equipment, military paintings and early military post artifacts. A polished brass gatling gun sits in the middle of the room.

(exhibit) **THE POST TRADER'S STORE** is a *practical set* completely furnished with reproduction trading goods such as flour, candles, crackers, soap, blankets and tinware. In an adjacent room there is a retail outlet for gift items and books relating to the cavalry and the buckskinning trades.

(food) **THE POST BAKERY** has period confections for sale: fresh baked bread, cookies, pies, cakes, candies, and even *hardtack*.

(exhibit) **THE GUARDHOUSE** is a *practical set* containing a furnished jailer's quarters with bed, writing desk, holding cells and a solitary confinement cell.

(museum) **THE OFFICER'S QUARTERS** is a *practical set* and museum completely furnished in elegant Victorian furniture and antiques typically found in the quarters of the Officers commanding the western forts. Officers would have nice things shipped from the East to try to make the forts feel more like home.

(exhibit) **THE ENLISTED MEN'S BARRACKS** is a *practical set* of reproduction beds, footlockers, and trooper equipment. A huge iron stove sits in the middle of the room, a checker board sits on a handmade wooden table and uniforms hang on wooden pegs by each bunk.

(drink) **THE ENLISTED MEN'S BAR** is the place to go after a day on the dusty trail. Here the guests can "cut the phlegm" with non-alcoholic, uniquely-concocted soft drinks like *Green Whiskey, Corn Licker, Red Dog,* or the powerful *Tanglelegs,* a drink that'll tie your toes in knots!

(ride) **THE QUARTERMASTER'S CORRAL AND STABLE** is where the horses, feed and tack are housed for the troops. It is a period "set" for use in movies, and stables the horses used for regular **trail rides.**

(food) **THE POST KITCHEN AND MESS HALL** serves such delicacies as beans, soup, stew, hash, cornbread and fritters, meatpie, smoked venison or buffalo, and fresh vegetables from the company garden. And the meals are served in trooper mess kits! The preparation of all foodstuffs adheres strictly to Army regulations.

(gifts) **QUARTERMASTER SUPPLY** is the source for reproduction Civil War and Indian War uniforms and accoutrements. Re-enactors will find frock coats, great coats, shell jackets, trousers, hats, insignia, canteens, haversacks, tents, camp furniture, holsters, cartridge boxes, guns, swords, battle flags and much more.

(exhibit) **OTHER BUILDINGS AT THE FORT** include the *Powder Magazine, Granary, Hospital, Blacksmith's Shop, Carpenter's Shop, Laundress's Quarters* and the *Post Cemetery*.

EXISTING FORTS FOR STUDY: Below is a list of forts and trading posts run by national and state parks that have been restored or reconstructed and are a good source for viewing authentic interior furnishings and living history demonstrations.

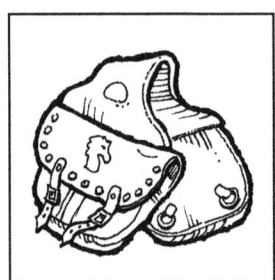

Fort Laramie, Fort Laramie, Wyoming.
Fort Scott, Fort Scott, Kansas.
Fort Davis, Fort Davis, Texas.
Fort Totten, Fort Totten, North Dakota (stone construction).
Bent's Old Fort, La Junta, Colorado (1834, adobe).
Fort Bridger, Fort Bridger, Wyoming (1843, stone).
Ft. Langley, British Columbia, Canada.
Fort Hall, Pocatello, Idaho.
Fort Clatsop, Astoria, Oregon (1805, logs).
Fort Nisqually, Tacoma, WA (1832, logs).
Fort Vancouver, Vancouver, Washington.
Presidio La Bahia, Goliad, Texas.
Cove Fort, Cove Fort, Utah.
Fort Ross, Jenner, California.
Sutter's Fort, Sacramento, California.
Fort Parker, Groesbeck, Texas.
Fort Michilimackinac, Mackinaw City, Mich.
Fort Snelling, St. Paul, Minnesota.
Fort Sisseton, Lake City, South Dakota.
Fort Churchill, Silver Springs, Nevada.
Fort Osage, Sibley, Misouri (1808, logs).
Fort Stanwix, Rome, New York (1758, logs).
Mansker's Station, Goodlettsville, Tennessee (1783, logs).
Hubbell Trading Post, Ganado, Arizona (stone).

THE BROKEN SPUR
A Cattle and Horse Ranch

"[The cowboy is] just a plain, everyday bow-legged human, care free and courageous, fun-loving and loyal, uncomplaining and doing his best to live up to a tradition of which he is proud."

— Raymon F. Adams, *Western Words*

The life of the cowboy still fascinates young and old alike—the songs, the stories, the adventure and excitement; stories of courage, loyalty and determination—but what was life on the range really like? The *Broken Spur* is a typical mid-western cattle rancher's homestead with its **Main House** where the owner's family lives, the **Bunkhouse** for the hired hands, a **Barn** for hay, feed and horse tack, a **Corral** for breaking horses, and a **Smokehouse** and **Outhouse**. Every building is an authentically and historically detailed replica laid out so they can be used as movie sets, both inside and out. **Longhorn cattle** can be seen roaming the surrounding prairie.

(rides)   The **RANCH** is the trailhead for horseback riding into *The Territory's* "outback". Trail guides and park naturalists provide interpretive services to help guests understand geology, plants, animals and the history of "the valley". Many kinds of wildlife abound: elk, deer, javelina, jackrabbits, field mice, etc. Many varieties of cacti: yucca, prickly pear, devil's pincushion, ocotillo, century plant, etc. populate *The Territory*. One-hour and full-day trips are available, and **chuckwagon lunches** are part of the day trips. An early "breakfast ride" includes an authentic **cowboy breakfast** over a campfire.

(entment)   **EDUCATIONAL DEMONSTRATIONS** on ranch life occur regularly at the ranch: The guests participate in fence mending, soap making, quilting, "trick" roping, lariat making, horse shoeing, furniture making, butter churning and the cooking of sourdough bread. The real—not the legendary—life of the cowboy and his family is demonstrated here: riding fence, doctoring the animals, greasing windmills! A chuckwagon is always set up, its cookbox open to reveal the corn meal, flour, lard, chili powder, etc. used to prepare a

VIEW OF THE BROKEN SPUR RANCH

meal on the open range. The cook will tell the visitors about pranks he pulled on *greenhorns* in his day.

(entment) **NIGHTTIME ACTIVITIES** include **campfire singing** and music from a cowhand with a guitar and harmonica; songs like *I Ride an Old Paint* or *Poor Lonesome Cowboy.* **Storytellers** relate thrilling tales of grueling cattle drives, and sunset **hayrides** for young and old lovers alike will cap off an evening.

The ranch is built with a rustic "open-prairie" look with an extensive use of logs and heavy, handmade furniture and decorated Indian rugs. A short description of each main building is found below:

(info) **MAIN HOUSE:** The ranch headquarters and home to the rancher's family, it has a large, homey living, dining and office area with a large stone fireplace as a grand centerpiece. The kitchen - completely period furnished—is at the back of the house and the bedrooms are upstairs. The kitchen and interior bathroom have a newfangled running water system. "Dudes" wanting to purchase tickets for the trail rides—or just rest from the sun—are welcome here.

(exhibit) **BUNKHOUSE:** It's an austere room with rows of link-spring cots, a round table for playing cards, hooks for hanging clothes and a pot-bellied stove for warmth in the winter. On the clothing hooks, hang worn, sweat-stained, classic western hats (including *sombreros*), yellow slickers, cowboy cuffs, gauntlets, vests, and *chaparejos* (chaps). What is the difference between *woolies, batwings* and *shotguns*? Why did cowboys like to wear suit vests? This exhibit attempts to answer these kinds of questions in entertaining ways. It's also usable as a *practical set* for film crews.

(sleep) **BUNKHOUSE:** Overnight accommodations with a cowhand flair.

(exhibit) **BARN:** For housing and feeding the trail horses, it has a number of stalls, a feed room, a tack room and a hayloft with a "bird's-eye view" of the ranch complex. The **Tack Room** displays antique bridles, bits, saddles, lariats, spurs, bullwhips and saddle bags.

(entment) **CORRAL:** Built in a circular pattern out of logs tied together, this is where guests will find living history demonstrations on horse shoeing, cattle branding, and on special occasion, bronco busting. Kids are shown how to crack a bullwhip and throw a loop with a lariat.

(food) **THE COOK'S SHACK.** A long, narrow building that looks like just another bunkhouse is actually a "restaurant" for visitors to the ranch. Very long heavy wooden tables with long benches for seating, both indoor and out, is where guests can sit down for a plate full of down-home ranch 'fixins': not just *frijoles* and bacon or *"son-of-a-gun"* stew, but hickory-smoked barbecue from an open-pit grill: beef, pork, chicken, and or venison served with all the trimmings: potato salad, coleslaw and pickles. For dessert: homemade, hand-churned ice-cream AND lively music from a smokin' fiddler! Several wall hung glass cases display cowboy collectibles such as a collection of original tobacco pouches, a collection of pocket knives and watches, a *housewife* (sewing kit), and items for entertainment like playing cards, dice, concertinas and a Jew's harp. Kids'll get a chance to meet the old cantankerous ranch cook but they better be careful what they say about his vittles!

(exhibit) **OTHER OUTBUILDINGS.** Other furnished exhibits include the ranchhand's *"Six-holer" Outhouse, Windmill & Water Storage Tank,* and the *Milk & Meat House,* The smell of meats being cooked in the *Smokehouse* is one of those memorable experiences lost to today's urbanites.

RODEO ARENA: Outside the ranch house proper is a small "old-style" rodeo arena made of timbers tied together in a zig-zag fashion. Wooden bleachers are placed around the corral for guests to view a RANCH RODEO performance. Accomplished skills in roping and riding stout-bred, strong-willed horses became a necessity during the western cattle drive era. Along with that came a competitive spirit among the "cow punchers" who started **riding and roping contests** staged in the nearest available corral. Today's rodeo events evolved from skills required of the cowboy to tame their horses and manage their stock, like calf roping, saddle-bronc riding and team roping. The "ranch rodeo" at the *Broken Spur* is more of a demonstration of these skills than a full-fledged competition rodeo. Cowboys are not actually competing but are skilled horsemen putting on a show. There are none of the events that developed in the twentieth century, like steer wrestling and bull riding. The show might go on something like this: on horseback in the center of the arena is an old hand at ranching, a true dyed-in-the-wool cowboy with wide-brimmed hat, chaps, bandanna—all the trimmings. He is the host for a demonstration of horse and cattle handling, and will explain them to the audience sitting on bleachers around the small corral. Several cowboys ride in with a dozen range cows to demonstrate the skills of their well-trained quarterhorses as they "cut out" and separate the cattle from the herd, one by one. They then demonstrate the roping, tying, and branding of calves (simulating the actual branding with an iron that's PAINTED a glowing red!) A couple of lady cowhands demonstrate barrel racing—demonstrating the ability of their quarterhorses to make fast cuts and turns. The host spews out a few gripping tales about his adventures with the "little doggies". Then it's competition time: the "How Fast Can You Get Up And Ride" where "sleeping" cowhands must climb out of their bed rolls, roll them up, put on their boots, saddle their horse and ride off! Fastest cowboy wins (and saves the stampeding heard)! Other thrilling contests provide for a "high-time" at the ranch rodeo.

The *Broken Spur* **ranch** is about the cowboy. It took a lot of hardship to build a cattle kingdom. On a hard land, out in the open, with no protection from the elements, they kept up their spirits, developing music and humor to fight the solitude of life on the plains. They had to raise families in a wild land where they had to make what they needed, and repair what they had. *RedRock Canyon Territory* tries to cut through the legends and develop an understanding for what it really was like to make a living in the frontier West.

EXISTING RANCHING MUSEUMS FOR STUDY:
The National Ranching Heritage Center, Lubbock, TX.
Hovander Homestead Park, Ferndale, Washington.
Saver-Beckman Farmstead, Stonewall, Texas.
Grant-Kohrs Ranch N. H. S., Deer Lodge, Montana.
Living History Farms, Des Moines, Iowa.
Bradford Brinton Memorial Ranch, Sheridan, Wyoming.
George Ranch Historical Park, Richmond, Texas.

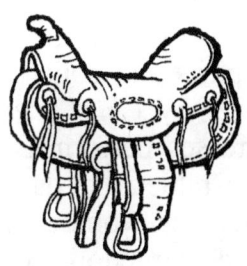

Silvercliff, Colorado

HEAMMAWIHIO
An Indian Encampment

"My people are few. They resemble the scattering trees of a storm-swept plain . . . there was a time when our people covered the land as waves of a wind-ruffled sea covers its shell-paved floor, but that time long since passed away with the greatness of tribes that are now but a mournful memory."

— Seattle (on surrendering land for city, 1855)

Nestled up against the magnificent *Twin Buttes* outcropping in *Dagger Flat* is a re-creation of a southwestern Indian village, with its numerous buffalo tepees, thatched lean-tos, ceremonial campfire, skin drying racks, and blanket weaving looms tied between trees. (*Heammawihio* is Cheyenne for "The wise one above".)

(museum)   **INDIAN CAVE MUSEUM.** Enter a small cave opening in the side of twin buttes, and in a large cave interior, guests will find on display authentic Indian artifacts to ponder: clothing, ceremonial objects, recreational equipment, tepee furnishings, tools, weapons and musical instruments. There are hand-painted buffalo robes, baby cradle boards, ceremonial pipes, mittens, rattles, ornaments, warrior shields, cookware, etc. There is also information and displays on the life of the American Indian in the nineteenth century: hunting techniques, village life, religion and warring with other tribes.

(demo)   **TRIBAL CEREMONIES.** Living history activities by Indians in period costume occur regularly in the village. Observe the tribal custom of "making medicine" to appease the spirits and solicit their aid, or watch a medicine-man ritual resided over by *Chief Speckled Snake*. Costumed dancers with elaborate headdresses perform for the casual guest. Guests might witness a rainmaking rattlesnake dance or *Divine Sun* dance. In addition to the ceremonies, the women of the tribe demonstrate, hide tanning, cooking, tipi construction, sewing hides, making pottery, basket and blanket weaving, and decorating with porcupine quills. Hand-crafted Indian goods from American reservations are available for sale in *Diablo*. Guests of *Heammawihio* will also see sign language demonstrated along with how to raise and lower a tepee.

INDIAN VILLAGE RE-CREATIONS: Pawnee Indian Village, Republic, Kansas (1830's, site). **Cherokee Heritage Center**, Tahlequah, Oklahoma (late 1800's).

PART IV: THE RAILROAD

RAILROAD INTERLOCKING TOWER, NEAR DEVIL'S RIVER BRIDGE

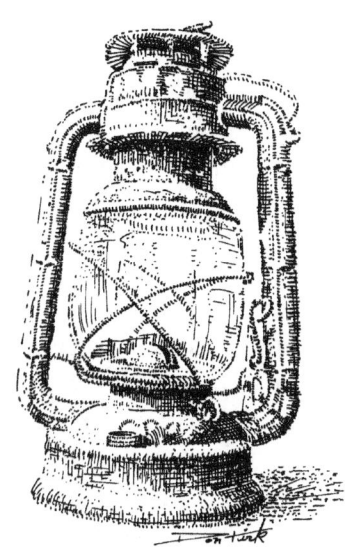

WESTERN RAILROAD
Entertainment

"Come the gaugers, spikers, and bolters, and a lively time they make of it. It is a grand 'anvil chorus' . . . in triple time, three strokes to the spike, 10 spikes to a rail, 400 rails to a mile, 1,800 miles to San Francisco."
— W.A. Bell, reporter with *Union Pacific* construction crews, c1868.

This chapter discusses structures, museums, entertainment, food and accommodations related to the *Wagon Wheel Gap, Tincup & Diablo Western Railroad*. As mentioned earlier, depots of various designs are found at each town in **The Territory** served by the railroad. The main working yard with service facilities is located near *Wagon Wheel Gap* along with the railroad's "Engine House Museum" discussed later in this chapter.

THE RAILYARD. Every railroad needs a switching and maintenance yard and the *W. W. G., T. & D. Western Railroad* is no exception with its *Roundhouse, Turntable, Machine Shop, Water Station, Coaling Tower* and *Sand House*. The yard is alive and working to keep the steam engines running and the right-of-way maintained. In the yard, are also some antique rolling stock and railroad equipment for guests to explore.

THE BUZZARD'S ROOST RAILROAD HOTEL. Early railroad hotels placed near the tracks at rail junctions were designed for train passengers who had to stay the night to catch connecting trains. The *Buzzard's Roost* is a two-story hotel in the design of a turn-of-the-century railroad hotel with views of the railyard from the windows of each room. Guests can get up early to watch the yard come alive as steam locomotives and cars are readied for the day's runs. The lobby has a check-in counter in one corner with a key rack on the wall and numerous signs describing the rules of the house. A huge grandfather clock stands near the counter. A china cabinet displaying railroad memorabilia sits on an opposite wall with hair-raising stories of railroading available just for the asking. The portraits of *C.P. Huntington* and *Thomas C. Durant,* the men who built the first transcontinental railroad, hang on the wall. A pot-bellied stove stands idle near the door, ready to go to work on a chilly morning. The rooms are small and unimposing: wood-frame beds with cozy comforters, a washbasin in the corner, and a small "chest of drawers". The entire hotel serves as the parlor: a dining room for a continental breakfast and for writing postcards home; a large lobby for reading and talking to new guests, a swing under an old pecan tree, and the entire town of *Wagon Wheel Gap* to explore until dinner time.

THE HARVEY HOUSE. "Wanted: Young Women of Good Character, Attractive and Intelligent, 18 to 30" —ad for Fred Harvey girls. This restaurant is *Fred Harvey's* improvement over the indigestion from railroad lunch stops that preceded it. In the 1880's *Frederick Henry Harvey* became the food concessionaire for the *Santa Fe* railroad and for the first time made a railroad famous for its good food. He also improved the service by adding waitresses that became known as "Harvey Girls". The *Wagon Wheel Gap Harvey House* is a first-class station-stop lunch cafe with these "Harvey Girl" waitresses in uniforms. A lunch counter with revolving stools and round dining tables, with the finest railroad china, fill the high-ceilinged cafe. Wood-planked floors, a pressed-tin ceiling, and a forest of posts supporting the ceiling, add charm and nostalgia to the meal. Menu items include steaks, fish and venison and are identified with railroad slang names: the *"Fishplate"*, the *"Bogie"* sandwich, the *"The Crummy"* cream cheese pie, etc. And, of course, guests can get *"Mulligan Stew"*, the gourmet treat of the celebrated railroad Hobo!

The ICE HOUSE is a WAX MUSEUM architecturally designed after a railroad trackside icehouse: railroads found it advantageous to build their own icehouses because of their large consumption of ice at depots, offices, shops, and passenger cars, and a lot of ice was needed for preserving perishable freight. The building is timber-frame construction with slick, wood plank floors and double walls filled with insulating wood shavings. Doors to the building are stacked above each other, in order to access the ice. An old hand-operated freight elevator, hanging on pulleys, sits in one corner of the building. The place is cool and mysterious, the perfect place to harbor **wax figure displays** depicting events in American railroad history. Chilling sounds are used to animate the displays, like that of an impending train wreck with approaching trains heard tooting their steam whistles in panic. Dioramas such as Chinese workers building the Transcontinental, railroad Barons discussing business in a Pullman car, and surveyors sighting in a route are found in this eerie wax museum.

RAILROAD HOTELS FOR STUDY:
Old City Park, Dallas, Texas
Kingman, Texas
Sanderson, Texas
RAILROAD DEPOTS FOR STUDY:
Hillsboro, Texas; **Burton**, Texas; **Ranching Heritage Center**, Lubbock, Texas; **Virginia City**, Nevada; **Chama**, New Mexico; **Minnehaha Depot**, Minneapolis, MN; **Leadville**, CO; **Sierra Blanca**, Texas; **Silverwood Theme Park**, Silverwood, Idaho; **Old Tucson Studios**, Tucson, Arizona; **Marathon**, Texas.

On The Train
ENTERTAINMENT

"The railroads had an incomparably romantic appeal, far beyond mere transportation. Railroad travel exercised a charm upon the human spirit."

— Phyllis Zauner, *The Train Whistle's Echo*

The **W.W.G.,T.&D. Western Railroad** is not just transportation between towns in *RedRock Canyon Territory*. Living historians in nineteenth-century period costume provide color, interest, and adventure to the train ride experience around *The Territory*. Entertainment would be provided by local area musicians, comedians, actors, and living history re-enactors. The rail cars would be sprinkled with fascinating characters from the nineteenth-century American West:

1) The **NEWS BUTCH** of the 19th and early 20th century roamed the trains peddling the necessities of travel for passengers trying to endure the long arduous trips. The acting company could re-create this character in an entertaining way. He could actually be selling soft drinks, sarsaparilla, candy, fruit, salted peanuts, and a period newspaper that would provide interesting reading about the area history. The *News Butch* would also carry the other things he would be trying to hawk if this was a real 19th-century trip: tin cups, sugar, coffee, cigars, towels, soap, and racy books like the *Police Gazette*. All the essentials for an arduous cross country rail trip! The actor's banter would explain the need for these things and by doing so teach a bit about what it was like to ride a train in the Early American West.

2) The **CARD SHARK** saw a place to fleece the naive Eastern travelers. He too would roam the train trying to entice passengers into a game of three-card monte. In typical gambler garb, an actor would put on a show for small groups of passengers at a time, never actually taking any of their money, of course.

3) The **CONDUCTOR**, in full period costume—conductor's hat, navy blue suit with brass buttons and watch chain—would punch tickets, help the passengers with their comfort needs, and answer questions about the train and the passing scenery. The Conductor is also an actor who will participate in skits with the other players on the train.

PART IV-6   REDROCK CANYON TERRITORY © DON KIRK

4) The **TRAIN ROBBERS**, rough desperadoes brandishing pistols and shotguns, board the train to steal the cashbox and rid the passengers of their valuables. The train would not actually have to stop, the train would shudder and screech, and actors already on board would enter each car for the show. *Confederates* and *Westerners* already seated would participate in the performance. (The same actors could replay the skit for each car.)

5) The **WAY PASSENGERS** were the real Westerners who rode the train from station to station carrying on their daily business in the West. They would be farmers, fur trappers, cowhands, miners, and even Indians. They were undoubtedly a fascinating sight to the Easterners, and so too, they would be captivating to our guests coming from out-of-state and other countries! Each would be a visual joy to see, and each actor would play to the profession he is exhibiting.

6) **MUSICAL ENTERTAINERS** pass through the cars, stopping in each car to sing a song or recite a poem. Carrying their banjo, harmonica or accordion they would sing about cattle drives, *Casey Jones*, and romantic train wrecks.

The Westbound Limited cannonballing past Chaco Station

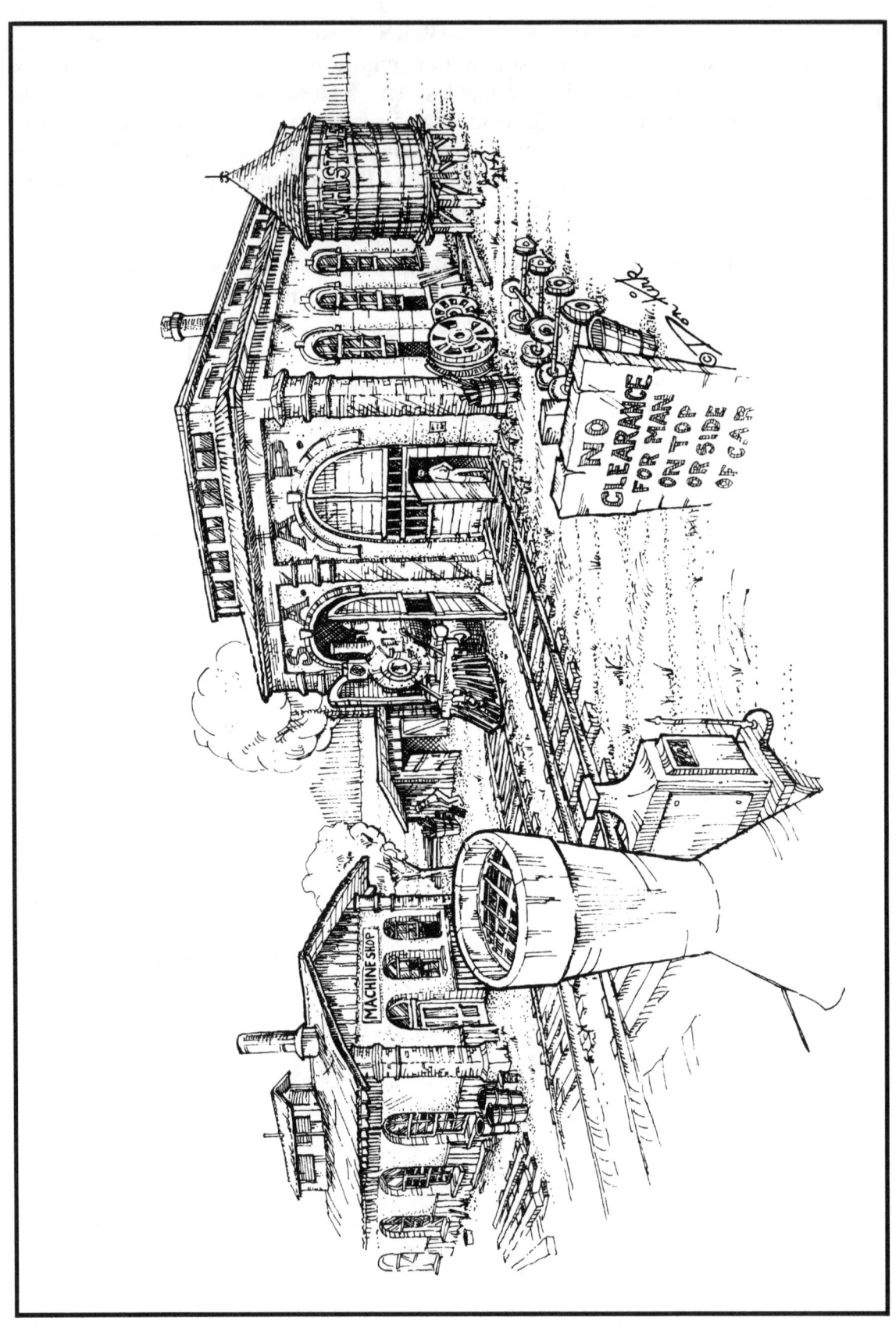

THE ENGINEHOUSE MUSEUM AT WAGON WHEEL GAP

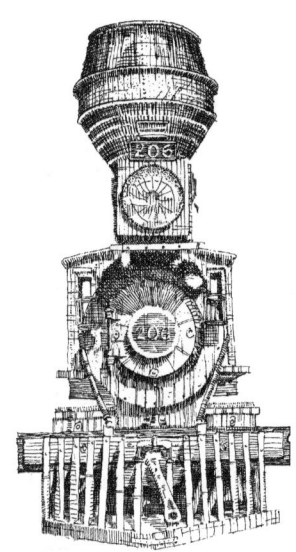

The ENGINEHOUSE MUSEUM

"There is a special quality to the light inside locomotive sheds, buildings which have been called the 'cathedrals of the industrial revolution' —though a hellish atmosphere of sulfurous smoke and oily steam envelopes these resting monsters."
— David Bourne

Across the tracks from the town of *Wagon Wheel Gap* is a railroad museum designed as an 1880's narrow-gauge **railroad maintenance facility**, though built on a much smaller scale. It consists of several buildings: an **engine shed, machine shop, supply depot, handcar house** and **tool shed**. In the yard sit rows of pony wheels, engine parts, worn passenger seats, driving wheels, and other repair parts. The museum is separate from the actual buildings used by the parks railroad, but it is placed in close proximity to the working yard and appears to be a part of it. Guests can access the museum safely without crossing active track.

ENGINE HOUSE. Set up in a tall, red brick building with green bay doors—a reproduction of an old engine shed—is a museum that pays tribute to the men who built and worked on the railroads: the switchmen, brakemen, telegraphers, conductors, firemen, engineers, station agents, surveyors, "rust eaters" and graders. With contemporary photographs, antiques, and dioramas, the process of laying and repairing track is demonstrated. The firing up of a locomotive, full scale "sections" of the boiler, etc. are shown. The daily lives of *The Brotherhood of Railroad Workers* is shown in pictures, video and sound.

MACHINE SHOP. A "Safety First" sign hangs over the door. Entering this building, guests can experience a period reconstruction of a shop for fabricating and repairing steam engine parts. Early machining equipment is on display: drill presses, lathe machines, grinders, shapers, etc. As a late nineteenth-century machine shop replica, the individual machines are all run by a single steam engine connected to a shaft that runs across the top of the machine room. Wide flat belts run from pulleys on the shafts down to each machine. Here also, the visitor will find railroad antiques like oil cans and lanterns, boiler plates and steam gauges. The **Master Mechanic's Office** is at the corner of the building and is a diorama with a "mannequin" working at a desk piled with papers. Greasy fingerprints cover the papers. Many kinds of skills were required to maintain the locomotives and cars: machining, pipe fitting, blacksmithing, carpentry, and tin-smithing—so tribute is paid to the craftsmen who kept the trains rolling.

SUPPLY DEPOT. A small adjoining building is a storeroom for railroad expendables. Cleaning materials like brooms, mops, pails, and scouring powder. Wooden bins contain bolts, rail spikes, screws, and nails. Shelves hold cans of lubricating oil and lanterns. A large bin holds coal for fuel. A small desk sits in one corner with racks nailed to the wall, organizing the paperwork. This exhibit pays tribute to the employees whose job it was to supply the railroad with the necessities.

HANDCAR HOUSE & TOOL SHED. Next to the "main line" with a pair of rails leading from the track to a wide door, the handcar house stores just that: a *handcar* used to carry the section gang down the line to do repairs. Another building adjacent to it houses tools and rail fittings (like *fishplates* and rail spikes). Guests can peer in to these exhibits.

WATER TANK & PUMPHOUSE. Setting just to the south of the main depot, a 100 yards or so, this railroad icon allowed the tender to be filled while passengers were disembarking at the station. A well was dug here to retrieve inexpensive water, though this water with all its inherent minerals, would quickly corrode engine boilers. A small steam driven pump would draw the water until replaced by oil engines, and later replaced by electric pumps.

A 1925 2-8-2 taking on water near the village of Muckwater

OTHER R.R. STRUCTURES IN THE TERRITORY

STOCK PENS. Out on the range are nineteenth-century stock pens built of rough-hewn timbers with a CHUTE to get the cattle into the stockcars, a WATER TROUGH to keep the cows fresh, and a 5 X 7 foot SHANTY for the managing cowhand to stay in during inclement weather. An old stockcar sits ready to take on Texas longhorns. If a guest peeks through the slats of the car he'll see a longhorn (actually a full-scale stuffed animal). Real longhorns "roam the range" in *The Territory*; sometimes a few can be found in the stockpens.

RAILROAD SECTION HOUSE. It was essential that track crews live on their assigned section, or as close to it as feasible, so they could always be on hand in case of emergencies and, of course, reduce lost time going to and from work. Thus, where the railroad passed through sparsely settled districts, section houses had to be built by the railroad for it's employees. A reproduction of a two-story section house sits near the tracks. It is an economically built wood frame structure, roofed with tin and sheathed on the outside with vertical boards & battens. There are two large rooms on each floor with bunkbeds. A one-story room addition houses the kitchen and dining table. The house has outdoor plumbing (outhouse), a cistern for water, a wood stove for heat and a kerosene lantern for light to play dominos after a hard day. A stack of 36 foot long iron rails sits near the building, weeds growing up around them.

THE DONEGAN. An old wooden freight car with peeling paint sits near the tracks with its wheels removed. Wooden steps lead up to a personnel door that has been cut into the car. Some clothes hang out to dry on a line, crude curtains hang in small windows also cut into the side of the car. This is an outdoor "diorama" of an old box car that has been turned into a bunkhouse for use by *section gang* laborers.

OTHER RIGHT-OF-WAY STRUCTURES. Listed below are other railroad structures seen in the yard or along the railroad right-of-way and used in its maintenance. All are authentically recreated to a 1880's style and painted the official railroad colors.

> **Coal Tipple and Sand House** for feeding coal and sand to the locomotives.
> **Watchman's Shanties** (flag house, switch house) are found at "dangerous" points along the route.
> **Turnouts and Sidings** for switching operations. Some sidings have static displays of old railroad rolling stock.
> **Tunnels and Trestles** used to cross mountains, creeks and arroyos.

Other non-railroad structures seen between towns by passengers on the *W.W.G.T.&D. Western Railroad:*

Old Stone Ruins of a long forgotten stage stop and the sight of an Indian massacre.
Homesteaders Cabin on the plains, long sense abandoned.
Lone Windmills and watering holes.
Hay Barn sitting in a quiet pasture.
Tent Town is a couple of tents with wooden floors setup on a spur to service railroad crews building a line off in another direction. A barbershop, saloon, surveyors crew, and a land sales office inhabit the tents.

SOME RAILROADS FOR STUDY:
Cumbres & Toltec Scenic Railroad, Chama, New Mexico.
Durango & Silverton Narrow Gauge Railroad, Durango, CO.
Roaring Camp And Big Trees N.G. R.R., Felton, California.
Georgetown Loop Railroad, Georgetown, Colorado.
Laws Railroad Museum & Historical Site, Bishop, Calif.

Virginia & Truckee Railroad Co., Virginia City, Nevada.
Sierra Railway Company, Jamestown, California.
Nevada Northern Railway Museum, East Ely, Nevada.
Black Hills Central Railroad, Hill City, South Dakota.
Mt. Rainier Scenic Railroad, Elbe Washington.
Cass Scenic Railroad State Park, Cass, West Virginia.

An 1872 4-4-0 carries passengers around The Territory

SPECIAL EVENT RUNS
On The W.W.G.,T.&D.

With several parlor, dining, and passenger cars furnished in period decor, extra trains (called specials) will run on the **RedRock Canyon Territory** railroad for special entertainment events themed to attract specific groups of locals and tourists. Some of these Specials will be sponsored by clubs and non-profit organizations, others by **RedRock Canyon**.

1) Romantic **MOONLIGHT SPECIALS** and **VALENTINE'S DAY RUNS** scheduled to coincide with the full moon. Candlelight, a fine dinner, champagne, and a ray of moonlight shining in the train windows is all that is needed for a memorable evening.

2) The **ORIENT EXPRESS NIGHT TRAIN** starts with an evening dinner with the unexpected murder of one of the guest passengers ah la *Agatha Christi* style. It's a murder mystery train with the passengers roaming the train, interviewing suspects and looking for clues in an attempt to be the first guest to figure out "who done it" and win a prize. A small acting troupe performs the initial murder and members become some of the suspects with clues left scattered about.

3) A rolling **RAILROAD WEDDING** and reception. A must for all railroad buffs. One car is decorated as a chapel with an electronic organ that includes additional railroad sounds. Additional cars are provided for the reception. A still photographer or videographer comes with the package. Catering is done by a restaurant in the ***The Territory***.

4) An **ANTIQUE AUCTION TRAIN** loaded with antiques to be bid on by the passengers. The antiques are viewed in "box cars" on a siding before the trip. Those who want a chance to bid take the train for a trip down the line; snacks and drinks provided, along with a lecture by a well know dealer, art critic, or collector.

5) The **OUTLAW-LAWMAN SPECIAL** is for Old West buffs who enjoy studying the lawman, gunfighters and outlaws that became famous in the American West. Special guests host the trip (historians, fast-draw experts, western movie stars, etc.) as the group discusses

these men of fact and legend. New research and theories of historic gunfights are presented. Drink and meals are available. There already exists several national groups who could sponsor these special trains. An AMERICAN WEST or NATIVE AMERICAN special would be similar in nature but focus on some other aspect of American History. There are many American West associations that would be interested as part of their annual conventions.

6) The **TEENAGE FUN UNLIMITED** could be a wholesome, structured party for a high school graduation party, birthday party, or fiesta event set in the Old West with a variety of activities to entertain the group. Live musicians, magicians, games, and magical moments create a fun alternative to a night cruising the streets.

7) The **BACHELOR'S NIGHT OUT SPECIAL**. A bachelor party for men (or women) with food, drink, music, poker, and hurdy-gurdy girls!

8) The **FIELD TRIP SPECIAL**. American history and civics classes from area schools take a day trip around *The Territory* to explore American West history. The train stops at points along the line where geography and western daily life can be explained by historians in period costume. Ranching operations, homesteading, mining, etc. are discussed.

All aborad for the next town down the line

PART V: THE REST OF THE STORY

POSTER FOR A CHUCKWAGON COOKOFF

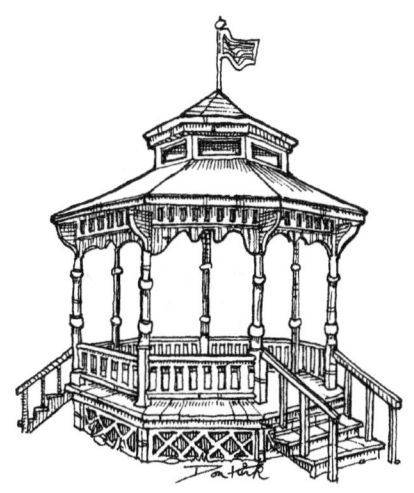

SPECIAL EVENTS
In The Territory

"There'll be a hot time in the old town tonight!"
— From the song "Hail, Hail, The Gangs All Here"

Most theme parks are designed for spectators only, to sit and watch a stage show, to take a 45 second amusement ride or walk down crowded, asphalt-paved streets to shop for souvenirs. But in *RedRock Canyon Territory* guests are invited to "live" and participate in the Old West. It is people that made the American West and it is people that will make *RedRock Canyon Territory* a living, breathing, re-creation of a western community with a flavor unique and different from today's theme parks and resorts. Guests become a part of the show, donning "costumes" and participating in regular and special events.

REGULAR EVENTS

There are numerous special activities that occur in *The Territory* on a regular basis. Listed below are some of them. Some are explained in more detail in other areas of the proposal.

SATURDAY NIGHT SOCIAL DANCE. Only period dances are played out here but there is always someone to teach the newcomers.

SUNDAY AFTERNOON BASEBALL GAME. Played by competing teams, in period impressions, just as it would have been played when it was first becoming an American pastime.

SATURDAY MORNING GUN SHOOTING COMPETITION. Shooting matches by professionals and amateurs alike using bottles and targets of the era.

OVERNIGHT TRAIL RIDES. Group trips into the "wilderness" with overnight camping and campfire cooking.

CHILDREN'S PROGRAM. A program for school children that allows them to spend the day in a structured program leaning about life in the frontier west.

REDROCK CANYON TERRITORY © DON KIRK

COURTROOM TRIALS. Actual historical trials are reenacted in the saloons and courthouses of *Wagon Wheel Gap*.

NIGHTLY OPERA HOUSE SHOWS. Re-creation of period plays and "vaudeville" shows. See the chapter "Live Entertainment at W.W.G."

WESTERN MOVIES. Shown at the *Nickelodeon* are early silent westerns and at the *Badlands Moving Picture Palace*, big "CinemaScope" westerns.

MOVIE LOCATION TOUR. Guests can go "behind the scenes" to visit a movie soundstage, property room, wardrobe department, production office and carpentry shop.

ANNUAL AND SPECIAL EVENTS

Can you imagine celebrating a special holiday in another place, in another time period? Everything looks, feels, sounds and tastes of another era. The host's are dressed in period impressions, the activities are performed the way they were over 100 years ago. It is a new kind of fun presently known only to living history groups and executed on a small scale such as period dances and Civil War battles. *RedRock Canyon Territory* provides a PLACE for large re-creations of historical and everyday events of the American West.

INDEPENDENCE DAY, WASHINGTON'S BIRTHDAY and **FOUNDER'S DAY.** Holidays were enthusiastically celebrated by townspeople and settlers alike. Families from all walks of life came together for these celebrations. Food and games were the order of the day. Horse races, baseball games, picnics, parades, shooting matches demonstrating fast draws and gun stunts, and "ugliest dog" contests were just the beginning of a memorable day. Calliope music might permeate main street. Games would include sack races, greased pig or greased pole contests, pumpkin-pie eating contests, jump roping, hoop rolling, wood chopping and wild footraces. There might be an ice-melting contest where guests wager on the melting time of a 150 pound block of ice sitting in a July sun. And in the evening there would be drinking, dancing and fireworks. Guests will be encouraged to come dressed in period costume, as *RedRock Canyon Territory* tries to re-create an authentic old-fashioned, family-oriented 4th of July and President's Birthday, an experience almost totally lost to today's generation of kids.

BATTLE AND GUNFIGHT REENACTMENTS. Living history associations are invited to use *The Territory* for historical reenactments of actual battles from the Texas Revolution, Mexican War, Civil War and Indian War campaigns. Re-enactment groups often have a problem finding a suitable location to put on special events where the public can see a bit of history replayed. **RedRock Canyon Territory** provides that place. Offices, storage facilities and other services like pyrotechnics, wagons and props are provided. No other site would be so conducive to a period atmosphere where the modern world with cars and powerlines destroy the authentic feel of the show.

ANNUAL BUCKSKINNING RENDEZVOUS. Based at the *Fort Carson Frontier Outpost*, modern day mountain men and their families come from around the country to re-create the fur trading era of the 1700's. Dresssed in buckskins and beads, sleeping in lean-tos and teepees, they compete in sports such as tomahawk and fry-pan throwing.

OLD WEST CHRISTMAS CELEBRATION. The town of *Wagon Wheel Gap* is, once a year, all lit up with kerosene lamps and decorated with handmade crafts. A huge pine tree stands in the town square. The smell of traditional foods, pastries and candies permeate the evening air. Little shops and stands sell hand-crafted toys and Christmas-tree decorations. Everything is done to re-create a European-styled Christmas imported to America by the early emigrants.

ANNUAL BARBECUE AND CHILI COOKOFF. Once a year the streets of *Wagon Wheel Gap* are filled with the smells of outdoor cooked food as contestants from all over the country compete to prove they have the greatest recipe.

TEXAS JACK STAR'S WILD WEST SHOW. Re-created at the rodeo grounds is a late nineteenth-century Wild West Show with buckskin-clad scouts, sharpshooting cowboys and war-bonneted Indians. *Buffalo Bill Cody* led the West in spectacular arena entertainment, but there were hundreds of imitators all putting on extravagant shows of marksmanship, horsemanship and frontier daring-do. *Texas Jack Star's* is one of those shows: a glitzy show of trick-shot artists: cowboys in ten-gallon hats, *woolies*, sequined jackets, and gleaming spurs. They are so gaudily dressed up, they bear little resemblance to real ranch hands. The late nineteenth-century shows were entertaining, action-packed spectacles that glorified and romanticized the West, further setting in concrete the Western myth. The West of legend is re-created for your enjoyment: Indians attack a stagecoach full of passengers, *Annie Oakley* rides the back of a buffalo, and *Wyatt Earp*, standing atop a galloping horse and brandishing two pearl-handled pistols, shoots at targets. Before every show **The Territory** is blanketed with colorful broadsides and handbills touting: "the grandest, most realisitic and overwhelmingly thrilling war-spectacle ever seen!"

EARLY TEXAS VAQUERO RODEO. On a regular basis, a mid-nineteenth-century rodeo is played out at the *Broken Spur Ranch*. Today's rodeo events evolved from the skills required of cowboys to tame their horses and manage their stock. Rodeos began because of a natural competitive spirit by the "cowpunchers" to start riding and roping contests staged in the nearest available corral. Guests can see this early cattle roping, saddle bronc riding and team roping without 20th-century rules and regulations and none of the events that were developed later, like steer wrestling and bull riding (more under *Broken Spur Ranch* rodeo).

INTERNATIONAL WESTERN FILM FESTIVAL. New films, foreign westerns and older classics will be shown at the *Badlands Moving Picture Place* and awards and honors given, not only to the filmmakers, but also to western actors and actresses. Western film stars and directors will host the festival. Historians will give workshops on various related topics.

WAGON WHEEL GAP ARTS AND CRAFTS SHOW. A town-wide art show and sale will exhibit western artist's current works: paintings, sculptures, ironwork, tinwork, furniture, pottery, and so forth related to the Old West.

MOONLIGHT RIDES BY RAIL AND STAGECOACH. On full-moon nights a special train serving dinners at sunset takes passengers on a moonlight ride around *The Territory*. Private stagecoach rides are available for young lovers of any age.

CONVENTIONS. Barbershop quartet organizations, reenactment and living history associations, buckskinning groups, historical organizations, fan clubs, and Western Art and Cowboy associations are invited to have conventions in **RedRock Canyon Territory**.

NON-PERIOD SPECIAL EVENTS might include beauty pageants, country and western band concerts, a one-act play festival and a custom rod and sports car show.

TRAIN SPECIALS. Extra trains are run on the *W.W.G.,T.&D. Western Railroad* for special events and conventions: murder-mystery trains, weddings, antique auctions, outlaw Specials, and more. For a detailed explanation see the chapter "Special Event Runs."

RedRock Canyon Territory is in no way a "theme park". It's a PLACE to have events that bring people together. It's a place already set up with the services and resources to sponsor, on a regular basis, special events in association with other organizations that promote and preserve a living history of our American past.

RESORT ASSETS
(Western Themed Resort)

"The enduring beauty of the West, free of restrictions and devoid of billboard advertising, will continue to appeal to a public that is increasingly hemmed in by the tensions and curtailments of modern living."
—George Fenin, *The Western* (1962)

The modern resort facilities of *RedRock Canyon Territory* are located in four perimeter areas of the park, over the hills, where they are beyond the view of filmmakers and guests. Nothing is visible in *The Territory* which might destroy the illusion of being in the Old West. Permanent residents have access to *The Territory* by way of a short stagecoach ride that takes them to the narrow gauge railroad (where they can reach any of the towns and villages in the park. All "day use" guests are shuttled to the main gate just outside *The Territory* at the *Wagon Wheel Gap* pass. The four resort villages of the park are called, *Sugarpine Falls, Cheyenne Wells, Stillwater Cove* and *Willow Springs*. Employees of the park can live in these villages or in cities on the outside of the park.

RETIREMENT COMMUNITY FOR MOVIE STARS

An important adjunct to *RedRock Canyon Territory* as a themed resort is the housing and services available for retired actors, directors, writers, artists, historians and craftspeople who love the Old West. Condominiums and cottages in the valley would be available for sale or lease to those stars who want a quiet place to reside and still be a part of the Old West. Housing would not be visible to filmmakers working in the valley but would be placed in small clusters in perimeter areas of the valley. Modern tennis courts, swimming pools, fitness centers, grocery stores, food services, etc. would be available along with easy access to the parks "Old West" features via the railroad and the stage lines. Members would also have their own direct access to the "outside world". Stars would be invited to participate in park activities of their choice, including "behind-the-scenes" activities such as doing research on the American West, collecting artifacts and antiques, student education programs, and public appearances. Those with "Old World" craft skills may work in the old towns demonstrating techniques to guests. Complete privacy would also be afforded celebrities, with no publicity or public tours of their private residences. The western actors could have a major influence on the success of **RedRock Canyon Territory**, as promoters and investors in the enterprise.

MODERN PERIMETER HOTELS

The hotels and boarding houses located WITHIN *The Territory* are authentic re-creations of late nineteenth-century accommodations. Because of that, the bath and water closet are located down the hall and air conditioning in the spring and fall would be by ceiling fans and open windows. So, for those guests who don't want to go that far in living the West, there are several hotels with modern conveniences situated in the hills surrounding the valley. They are designed with an "Old World" frontier west atmosphere but are NOT authentic re-creations of 1880's western town hotels: there are bathrooms in each room, central air-conditioning, swimming pools, and full hotel services.

CAMPING AND RV PARKS

There are three camping sites available for guests. One is an INDIAN VILLAGE with real tepees to sleep in and the second is a CAVALRY BIVOUAC with officer and enlisted wall tents laid out in rows. The third is a circle of settler's PRAIRIE SCHOONERS (wagons) with room to sleep a family in each one. Every night there are sing-a-longs and storytelling around the camp fire.

THEMED NIGHTCLUBS

After a long day in *The Territory*, guests who don't want to stay in the old towns for evening activities (opera shows, night street activities, etc.) may want to take advantage of the lively nightclubs in the resort areas of the park. Dancing, dining, drinking and live shows from "modern day" performers (bands, comedy shows, etc.) are set in unique modern decor with American West themes. One club might have western movie posters completely covering the walls with a movie screen showing western films. Another club might be set up as a country and western dance hall with a lighting and decor scheme to make it an adventure in dancing.

MOVIE RANCH ASSETS
(Western Movie Location)

"You do two things to make a good movie: you open it with a man galloping into town and end it with a kiss."
—John Ford

RedRockCanyon Territory is designed to work as an active movie location for shooting Westerns. The fact that westerns will be shot here is an important "draw" for western buffs and fans who will patronize the resort. Designed with the filmmaker in mind, *The Territory* will be a welcome place to shoot motion pictures. The available facilities and special characteristics of the park for making Westerns will include the following:

ONE: Numerous "PRACTICAL SETS" are already furnished with period antiques and reproductions with some "wild walls" and pull-out ceilings to allow for placement of camera, crew and lighting. Walls can be removed to enlarge the rooms and widen the views. Ceilings can be removed to reveal a lighting pipe grid or ceiling joists to hang lights on. Some of the practical sets in *Wagon Wheel Gap* were chosen based on their frequency of use in western films and include the saloon, Sheriff's office and jail, general store, bank, hotel lobby, school house, church, barbershop and livery stable. Most other buildings in **RedRock Canyon Territory** can also be used as "practical sets".

TWO: The towns, villages and structures in the valley are DESIGNED WITH THE CAMERA IN MIND. Besides the "art-directed" nature of the towns, the placement of windows, doors, balconies, set dressing, and so forth is such that cameras can be placed to shoot interiors with dramatic views of the town's streets outside. A *Steadicam* can easily move continuously from one interior, out to the street and back into another building without cutting. Exceptional views of the town and hill country beyond can be seen through these windows and doors. "Secret" stairs and mechanical elevators provide easy access for camera crew and equipment to upper story and ROOFTOP CAMERA PLATFORMS for high-angle views of the town streets and territory beyond. Some EXTERIOR "wild walls" afford views not obtainable in any other way. The Spanish Mission bell tower, church tower, the Victorian mansion's crow's nest, and other high points normally available to the general public are also designed for access by camera crews.

THREE: All buildings are complete PERMANENT STRUCTURES and not just building fronts, allowing exterior shots from any angle. There are no tilt-up building fronts without a structure behind them. Alleyways can be used as sets. Movie companies are invited to build such temporary fronts as needed for their production but they must be torn down or recycled after principal photography.

FOUR: The towns and villages are designed with EXPANSION in mind, making it possible for movie companies to build additional structures for their production. Any new permanent buildings built for a particular movie become part of the town and must be left standing. They must also meet certain guidelines in design and construction including the preservation of certain vistas and "picture points".

FIVE: *Wagon Wheel Gap* has been designed with CROSS STREETS AND VISTAS that make it possible to use it to represent more than one town in a single film. Numerous alleyways and plazas expand the possibilities even further.

SIX: *RedRock Canyon* has a number of other small VILLAGES, RANCHES AND STRUCTURES that can be used as sets, allowing the production company to shoot an entire film, or most of it, at this one location without having to pack up and move an entire production company. There's a Mexican village, mining camp, military fort, ghost town, cattle ranch, railroad yard, and more. What else could a director want!

SEVEN: The NATURAL LANDSCAPE FEATURES in the valley provide a number of typical western settings: canyons, arroyos, dry creeks, rock outcroppings, waterholes, desert landscape, cactus, mesquite trees, etc. *RedRock Canyon* is completely contained in a valley surrounded by hills; the nearest automobile traffic and city sounds are on the other side of a ridge. There are no airport flight lines over the property. Access by film crews with semi-trucks and mobile homes is over hard-packed dirt roads.

EIGHT: Located away from the main guest traffic areas is a SOUND STAGE COMPLEX with a stage that is fully insulated, sound deadened and air-conditioned, with built-in lighting grids and power drops. Large enough to contain several interior sets, it is hidden in *The Territory* where it will not interfere with guests enjoying the park, and film production crews can work undisturbed by "tourists". Partially buried and with a roof that is broken up to look like several separate buildings, it is invisible from the ground or air. Ground level docks and truck ramps allow easy access for camera, lighting, grip, prop and wardrobe trucks.

NINE: Some "in house" OFFICE SPACE AND FILM SUPPORT is provided for location production management people. A large PRODUCTION OFFICE is located at the SOUND STAGE COMPLEX and is fitted with several telephone lines, a copy machine, computer terminals and "storyboard walls". Available also, are walkie-talkies and mobile phones; all those things necessary for a location production company to function on location. Offices for the ACCOUNTING personnel, the DIRECTOR, LOCATION and PROPERTY DEPARTMENT are also provided. There is a small theatre that has an interlock projection system for showing DAILIES. Next to the sound stage is a space for WARDROBE: an area for sewing, distressing, storing costumes, and dressing extras, and a HAIR & MAKEUP room with mirrors, counter space and lighting.

TEN: A CARPENTER and PAINT SHOP near the sound stage is used at the resort to build most anything western. Also in *The Territory* is a period BLACKSMITH SHOP available for ironwork, and a working early-American SAWMILL that can produce rough-sawn timbers and planks that are absolutely authentic because of the way they are cut. A historical group of architects and carpenters, associated with the resort, provide expertise on early American building techniques.

ELEVEN: A high amperage ELECTRICAL DISTRIBUTION system is built into some of the practical sets where power from mobile, diesel generators is not practical. It is possible to just "plug in" sufficient lighting fixtures on the smaller "practical sets."

TWELVE: *RedRock Canyon* has its own WARDROBE DEPARTMENT for use by its living history employees and this would be available to film companies. The collection has "impressions" for any type of character that might be found in the Old West: buckskinners, gunfighters, storekeepers, cowboys, businessmen, outlaws, Indians, morticians, etc. A large assortment of hats, footwear, vests, coats jackets, shirts, pants, chaps, suspenders, ties, and neckerchiefs allow for many unique and interesting impressions. ACCOUTREMENTS are also available such as guns and leather goods (holsters, bandoleers and gunbelts).

THIRTEEN: An extensive "hand props" PROPERTY ROOM stores such things as tin stars, playing cards, poker chips, desk accessories, period stationery, etc. needed by actors for specific scenes. Larger props like trunks, barrels, camp cooking gear, and furniture can be found all around *The Territory* and pulled as needed for "set dressing."

FOURTEEN: HORSES and WAGONS used in the resort are also available to the filmmaker. To support the use of horses, *The Territory* has corrals and enclosed stalls, feeding and care facilities, saddles and horse tack, and skilled wranglers. A large assortment of reproduction and original wagons are used in the valley to haul supplies and passengers, and to use on static display around the town and villages. Buggies, chuckwagons, covered wagons, buckboards, stagecoaches and freight wagons are available to directors. Wagons can be used to carry camera equipment, reflector boards, etc., to keep modern tire tracks off the landscape and out of the shots.

FIFTEEN: *RedRock Canyon* is unique for "on location" shooting because it has a variety of OVERNIGHT ACCOMMODATIONS in the park that are ordinarily used for tourism. Several town hotels and guest ranches provide adequate space for both "above the line" and "below the line" cast and crew, saving companies hours of travel time transporting actors and crew to each days shooting location. RESTAURANT SERVICES are available to cater to the crew either in the restaurants or at the shooting sites.

Without a doubt, the multi-functional character of *RedRock Canyon Territory* as a movie set, museum and guest ranch is a "marriage made in heaven," *RedRock Canyon* strives, through careful management and planning by people with experience in each of the areas, to make it an enjoyable place for filmmakers to make their "greatest Western of all time."

EXISTING MOVIE RANCHES FOR STUDY:

Mescal, Old Tucson Studios, Benson, Arizona. (Private ranch)
    (*Young Riders* TV series)
Bittercreek, Bradshaw Ranch, Sedona, Arizona. (Private ranch)
    (*The Rounders, The Wild Rovers*)
Alamo Village, Happy Shahan Angus Ranch, Bracketville, TX. (Open to public)
    (*The Alamo, Two Rode Together, Bandolero, Barbarosa*)
Buckskin Joe, Canon City, Colorado. (Open to public)
    (*Cat Ballou, The Cowboys, True Grit, The Sacketts*)
Old Tucson, Tucson, Arizona. (Open to public)
    (*Arizona, The Last Outpost, Gunfight At The
    O.K. Corral, Joe Kidd, Posse, The Outlaw Josey Wales*)
Rancho Alegre, J. W. Eaves Ranch, Santa Fe, New Mexico (Private ranch)
    (*The Cheyenne Social Club, The Cowboys,
    Gambler Part III*)
Cook Ranch, Santa Fe, New Mexico. (Private ranch)
    (*Silverado, Gambler Part III, Desperado, Lonesome Dove*)
Disney's Golden Oak Ranch, Placertia Canyon, Hollywood, CA. (Backlot)
    (*Shenandoah, The Apple Dumpling Gang, Bonanza,
    Little House On The Prairie, Zorro, Paradise*)
Western Six Points, Universal Studios, Hollywood, California. (Backlot)
    (*Destry Rides Again, The Cimarrron Kid, The Shakiest
    Gun In The West, The War Wagon, The Virginian,
    Wagon Train*)
Columbia Ranch, Columbia Pictures, Burbank, California. (Backlot)
    (*The Lone Rider, High Noon, 3:10 to Yuma, Rin Tin Tin*).
Bordertown, Maple Ridge, British Columbia, Canada (Private ranch)
    (*Bordertown*)
Bonanza Creek Ranch Glen Hughes Ranch, Santa Fe, NM. (Private ranch)
    (*The Man From Laramie, The Cowboys, Silverado,
    Lonesome Dove, The Lazarus Man*)
Red Hills Ranch, Sedona, Arizona. (Private Ranch)
Apacheland, Apache Junction, Arizona. (Private Ranch)
RHS Studios, Spicewood, Texas. (*Redheaded Stranger*) (Private Ranch)

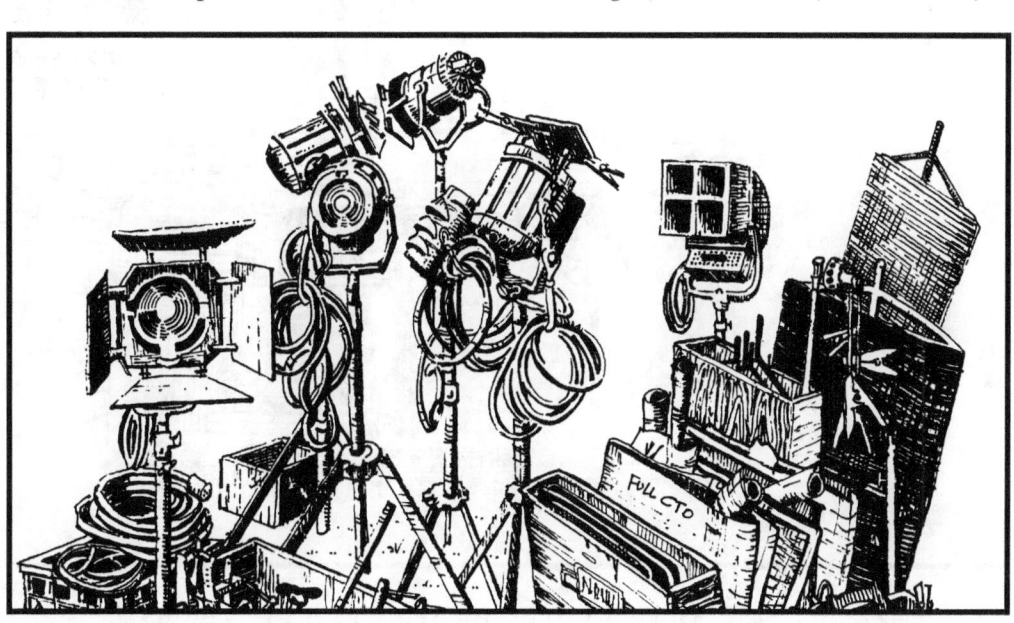

ALAMO VILLAGE, BRACKETVILLE, TEXAS

PARK ENTRANCE

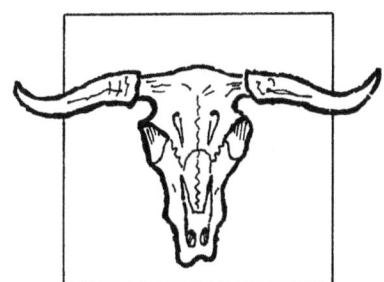

"Goodbye God, we're going to Bodie."
— Prayer by anonymous girl when she was told her family was moving to Bodie, California, a town know for its violence.

The PARK ENTRANCE is situated OUTSIDE the valley and is the "jumping off" place where the cars and the "outside world" come to a stop and the trip into the past begins. The narrow-gauge steam railroad is the only connection to the world of the "Old West". AUTOMOBILE PARKING is at the park entrance, several miles away from the Park. Only a narrow pass allows access into the valley (see map #0001). All supplies to *The Territory* (restaurant supplies, gift shop merchandise, etc.) is carried into the park by train or freight wagon (see more under "Park Transportation").

AVAILABLE SERVICES

The Park Entrance architecture is modern and there is no evidence as to the theme of the park. The buildings provide "transition services" for the guests:

> Ticket Purchasing.
> Costuming of guests.
> Purchasing of frontier money.
> Pet care kennels.
> Strollers and wheelchairs (period of course).
> Geriatric services.
> Locker rental.
> Restrooms.
> *Last Chance* souvenir gift shop for guests leaving the park.
> Emergency auto repair services.
> Transit services to the nearest major city.

GUEST DRESS

Guests are encouraged to come dressed to 'play the part' of a westerner. Hats, vests, etc. add to the atmosphere and authentic period feel of the park.

REDROCK CANYON TERRITORY © DON KIRK

Some days of the month will be set aside for guests who come fully outfitted in an Old West impression (their own or rented at the park entrance). This is a special day for still photographers who have a better chance of capturing "authentic" Old West scenes. Cameras are always welcome and encouraged in the park. Special leather "gun holsters" and "possibles bags" can be rented to carry the guest's still and video cameras so they can be hidden and "fit in" with the rest of the western outfit.

ADMISSIONS

Several customer options provide savings to guests by catering to their specific needs:

1. **DAY PASSES** are designed for out-of-town tourists and include general admission, a train ticket to the valley, and free unlimited rides within the park. Special events are not included.
2. **SEASON TICKETS** are available to local residents who plan to come back many times.
3. **FAMILY GROUP RATES** for one and two day general admission for families.
4. **TOUR AND GROUP RATES** for organizations and international travelers.
5. **SPECIAL EVENT TICKETS** are sold for special performances and holiday celebrations. Reenactment groups and non-profit living history organizations also perform historic battles that require separate admissions.
6. Guests who initially purchase only a **DAY PASS**, are given the opportunity to come back the next day for half-price.

NOTE: The number of guests in the park at any one time will be limited (except for special events) and on some days reservations may be required. The movement of guests from village to village around the park via train, stage, freight wagon or on foot allows more guests to enjoy the park without a feeling of being crowded (which is counter productive to the quiet and peaceful atmosphere strived for in the park). Nothing like the crowds found in other theme parks will be allowed in *The Territories* (except special event days, like the Independence Day Celebration, where "crowding" is a natural part of the event).

CURRENCY EXCHANGE SYSTEM

The park's **FRONTIER MONEY**, is an authentic reproduction of period bank notes and silver coins, issued by the *City Bank* in several denominations to be used as token money to purchase entertainments in the park (stagecoach rides, horseback riding, gold mine tours, opera house shows, food, haircuts, etc.) An effort is made to make the guest feel like they are "living" in the Old West of the nineteenth century. U.S. dollars would be converted to pre-inflation values. For example, 25 cents in *Frontier Money* will buy you a haircut in **The Territory** but you may have paid five 1992 dollars for that 25 cents. *Frontier Money* can be purchased in numerous places around **The Territory**: at the *City Bank* in *Wagon Wheel Gap* and at all railroad depots, saloons, and restaurants. Guest can also use their U.S. currency and credit cards most anywhere in the park. (The "Frontier Money" approach is intended primarily as a vehicle for the KIDS enjoyment and their learning to handle money. It allows the adults to control, and keep track of, how much the kids are spending).

MAINTENANCE AND SECURITY OPERATIONS

Security and maintenance is kept very low profile; hidden from view:

Security personnel are costumed as Marshals, Deputies, Pinkerton men and Cavalry Soldiers; some traveling the park on horseback.

Guest problems and complaints are addressed at the *Territorial Marshal's Office* in *Wagon Wheel Gap* and the *Sheriff's Office* or saloon in the other towns of *The Territory*.

Security's Main Office and Communication Center is hidden behind the *Marshal's Office* in *Wagon Wheel Gap*. Electronic security equipment and "shortcut passageways" lead to all parts of the town.

Maintenance and repair shops are hidden among the Old West architecture in different areas of the park. Used also are the 1880's sawmill at *Wagon Wheel Gap*, the carpenter's shop, railroad machine shop, and blacksmith forge found within the park.

EMERGENCY SERVICES are especially important because the park is in a secluded valley with normal transportation by steam train and stagecoach. To get patients out of the park quickly, **RedRock Canyon Territory** will have an on-site EMS crew and transport vehicle at *Wagon Wheel Gap* and a "Nurses office" in each village, for minor injuries.

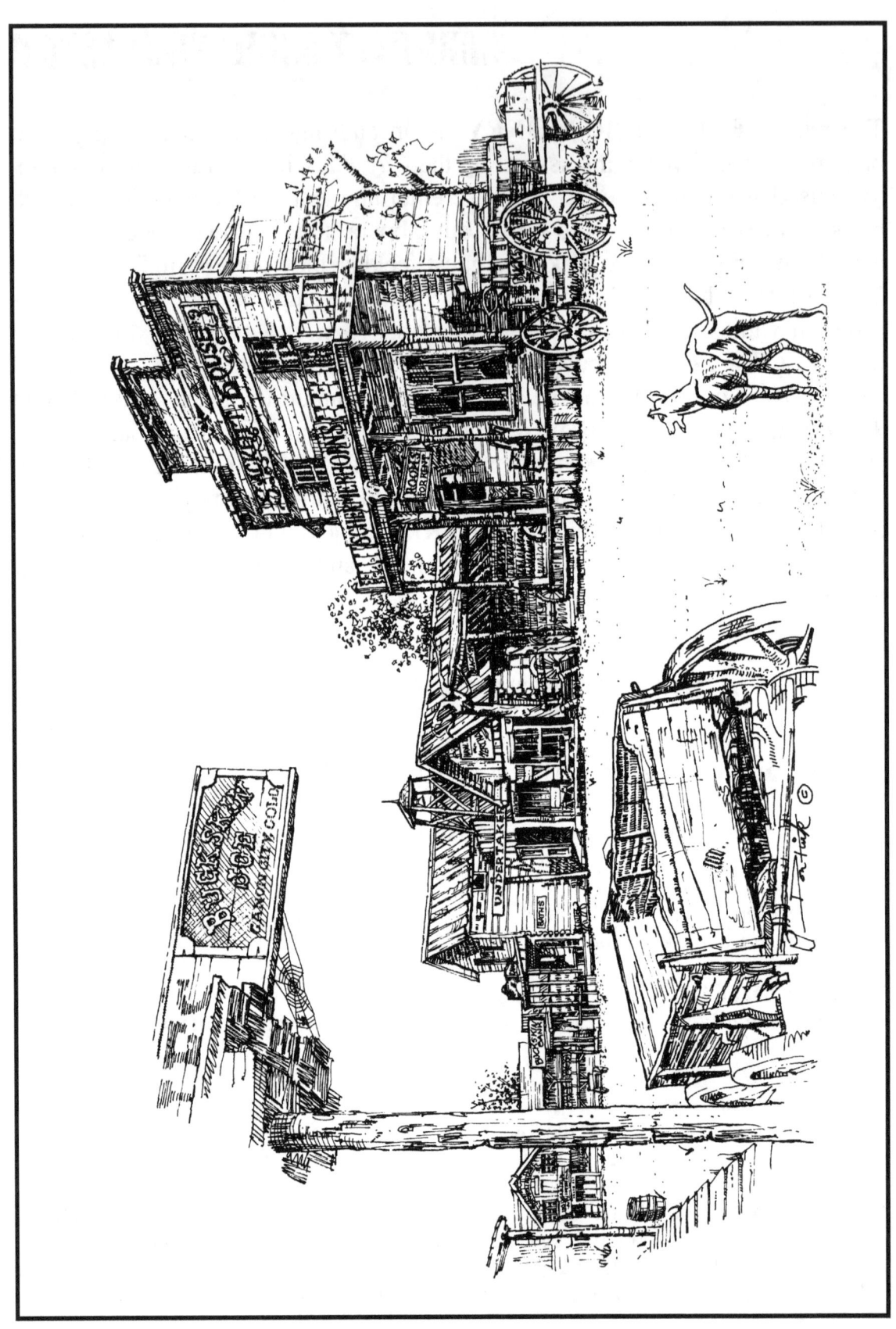

BUCKSKIN JOE, CANON CITY, COLORADO

INFRASTRUCTURE

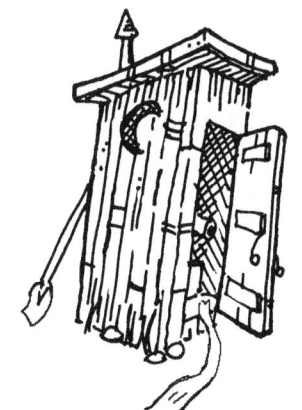

"I've always wanted to see the frontier . . . before it's gone."
— Kevin Costner, *Dances With Wolves*, 1990

ENVIRONMENTAL CONSIDERATIONS

The **park's relationship** to the surrounding cities and countryside is an important aspect in its design. Listed here are some of the design objectives of the park related to environmental considerations.

1. The park is designed to respect the land as a heritage to protect and pass onto future generations.

2. The park will coordinate closely with county and state governments for controlled economic development.

3. In designing the park, consideration will be given to the existing natural surroundings, to preserve all natural features and wildlife.

4. Water and sewage treatment, if economically feasible, will be handled through water wells and treatment plants within the park.

5. Electricity to supply the park's needs will come primarily from windmills and solarpanels within the park. Because of the "low-tech" nature of the park, not nearly as much electricity as the typical theme park will be required.

6. The resort will provide enough facilities for all guests without upsetting the environmental balance of the area.

7. All existing historical structures will be preserved.

With a STEAM RAILROAD and stagecoach being the only connecting transportation within the park, won't the coal or oil- fired engines be dirty and costly? And what happens if a steam engine breaks down?

A small diesel switch engine will always be available to replace a steam locomotive that has broken down. The smoke bellowing from the stack of an Iron Horse is the beauty of it as it crosses the landscape. When the fire is burning properly, this smoke is mostly white (steam); only on grades does the stack exhaust black cinders. Other tourist railroads running several trains a day have not had problems with the EPA. One or two trains will have to run continuously, though most of the time is spent loading and unloading passengers. Steam has an undeniable romanticism about it, adding immeasurably to the period feel of *The Territory*. Dozens of new tourist railroads have opened in the last few years with successful ridership.

INFRASTRUCTURE

All modern services are completely hidden from the guests and provide only those conveniences necessary for the needs of today's tourist.

1. ELECTRICAL DISTRIBUTION SYSTEM: Electricity is needed for Interior and exterior lighting, restaurant refrigerators, heating, air-conditioning, security and fire protection. A modern solar collection system using solarpanels and windmills, will be used throughout the park (*Arizona Mining World*, is a Western open-air museum that uses this method). An optional approach is using gas or coal generators, but that requires converting D.C. to alternating current where needed. Cooking will be done by butane gas where needed and emergency lighting will be handled with batteries. Movie companies will bring in their own mobile generators for lighting during filming, except in the case of the *Sound Stage Complex*, where commercial electricity will be brought in from outside. The *Murdock Mine* rides will also require commercial electricity. All power lines will be buried.

2. FIRE PREVENTION: Water mains, fire hydrants, sprinkler systems and fire extinguishers are hidden throughout each town. There will be an on-site volunteer fire department with a mobile tanker truck. All structures will have a hidden sprinkler system. Supply pipes are hidden in wooden box beams with the sprinkler heads sitting flush so they are barely visible. Six inch supply mains come from stock tanks in *The Territory*, fed by wind powered water wells and backed up by electric pumps. Three inch secondary mains are buried in the streets with fire hydrants hidden from view.

3. WATER SUPPLY SYSTEM AND SEWAGE DISPOSAL: Drinking water for guests, for restaurant cooking, restrooms, for fire prevention, and for livestock will be required. Several water wells run by windmills and/or electric pumps will supply water to *The Territory*. Cool drinking water is provided throughout the park free of charge (Guests will not be required to purchase drinks to prevent dehydration!) Hotels and food service establishments are also supplied with hot and cold running fresh water.

4. AIR CONDITIONING: A central air conditioning system in each village provides cool, filtered air to many of the buildings such as gift shops, hotels and museums (where temperature and humidity must by carefully controlled). The southwestern location of the park will eliminate any real need for heating systems.

5. MAIL SERVICES. A United States Post Office will be set up in the resort area of the park and basic postal services would be provided at *Wagon Wheel Gap*—the mail carried by *Pony Express* to the main post office.

6. TOWN LAYOUT: Buildings and grounds are laid out in such a way as to provide servicing and access passage ways between buildings for security, maintenance and supply activities.

NEW BUSINESSES ALONG THE RAILROAD

RELATED QUESTIONS

How are the ELDERLY GUESTS dealt with in *The Territory* proper where modern amenities are not apparent?

Special organized group tours are provided using "touring wagons" for transportation at certain points along the tour. Numerous modern restrooms with easy access are "hidden" throughout the park.

How is THE HANDICAPPED issue addressed in *RedRock Canyon* so that they are afforded an equal opportunity to participate in the activities of the park?

Special "touring wagons" designed to load and secure wheelchairs will run throughout *The Territory*. 1880's period-looking wheelchairs will be available so the guest will fit right in. Restrooms and most buildings will allow for wheelchair access.

How are INFORMATION AND ROUTING SIGNS dealt with in *The Territory*, such as restrooms, drinking water, security services, first aid?

Specific symbols for each facility would be designed that would "fit in" with the period setting and not standout appreciably. Signs wouldn't be placed on buildings in obtrusive ways as is so common in other parks. The same symbols would be placed on detailed maps of *The Territory* and the Motto "ask the nearest storekeeper for directions" will be promoted.

Will guests be willing to stay in the "19th-CENTURY" HOTELS that don't have the usual amenities?

Bed & Breakfast establishments and historic hotels have had a resurgence in popularity in recent years. Travelers are getting tired of the sameness of hotels wherever they travel. Going down the hall to the bathroom seems to be no problem, actually fun. Remember too, that these period hotels are located IN the period towns close to the action, and they have the VIEWS of *The Territory*.

How are MUSEUM COLLECTIONS dealt with in *RedRock Canyon*, when, to protect antiques, temperature and humidity must be carefully controlled?

The Museum buildings are modern insulated structures on concrete foundations, only the facades appear to be rustic, dilapidated period structures. Complete conditioning systems to control temperature and humidity are carefully camouflaged.

Won't the MOVIE HOUSES AND GIFT SHOPS in these period towns "break the spell" of being in the Old West?

Walking down the streets, they are hidden from view. Without these museums, movie houses and gift shops there would be little for the guests to do besides "soak up the atmosphere" and take pictures (a common problem with other western tourist towns). That's enough for western buffs, but not the general public.

Because the park is rustic and rugged by definition, how is the LIABILITY ISSUE addressed?

Actually risk of injury in *The Territory* may be LESS than traditional theme parks where the RIDES pose the most potential for serious injury. The dirt streets pose much less danger to children than asphalt streets which routinely skin up falling children. The trampling crowds at major theme parks are also a danger. Additional things that can be done include:

A "code of conduct" posted for guests to adhere to, discouraging "Horseplay" and use of intoxicants.

Guest could sign liability releases (assume some of the risks and be made aware of the dangers) and accept the dangers inherent in the activities at the park, "to the extent that these dangers are a necessary part of the activity and are obvious to the participant."

The park will work with legislators in the park's state to establish fair limitations on liability; determining where an 'amusement parks' responsibility ends and the guests begins.

The creative design and management team of *RedRock Canyon Territory* will strive to solve traditional theme park problems in new innovative ways.

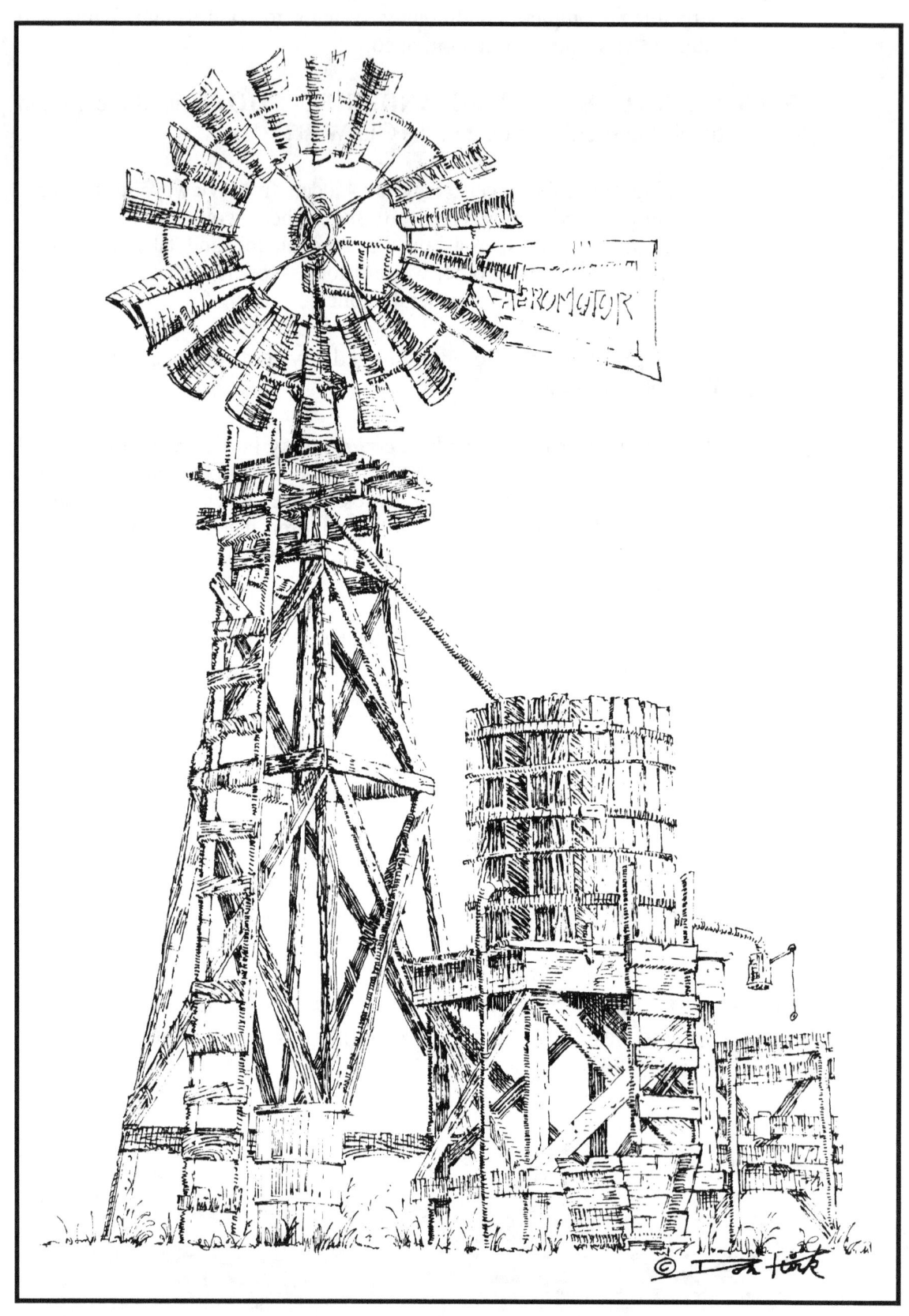

AN INVENTION THAT HELPED SETTLE THE WEST

SITE SELECTION

"In far too many cases, a project has started with the planner's acceptance of an unsuitable location. This is a cardinal planning error. An important, if not most important, function of a planner is the sometimes delicate, sometimes brutal task of guiding the entrepreneur to the selection of the best possible site for his project."
— John Ormsbee Simonds, *Landscape Architecture*, 1961

RedRock Canyon Territory is a blending of the natural landscape with man-made features to create a "themed park"—unlike a *Disneyland* or *SixFlags* where the park is constructed in a void—everything built from scratch, including rock outcroppings in plaster! The land is as much of the experience for guests as the man-made western towns: plants and animals, colors and textures, sounds, and the feel of the air. This makes the sight selection for ***The Territory*** a critical component to the success of this project.

Much of the parks physical design will grow out of the location of the selected site and its success will be very dependent on that selection. The site must be acquired before the project becomes known to the media.

The site must be protected from future modern development at its borders. Choosing a site adjacent to an exiting national or state park, BLM, or National Forest would provide the advantages of protected lands and would give filmmakers more virgin territory to shoot in.

> **The site must have a "western" landscape** with dramatic rock formations, distant mountains and desert vegetation. The landscape should vary within the property so the different towns can be appropriately sited to match their intended character and allow the one "territory" to represent many different areas in the western United States. Ideally, the site would have a 360 degree view of undisturbed landscape. Protection of the "period illusion" is best achieved by having the resort in a small valley surrounded by rugged hills that are controlled by the park. Many virgin areas can still be found all over the western United States. Arizona, Texas, Utah, New Mexico, Colorado, Nevada, California, Wyoming and Montana are all possible candidates, but other factors may eliminate some of them. For example, the site should be located in a climate that provides the longest

possible tourist and "shooting" season and it should be near a major city and along a tourist route. Possible locations must be searched out and then analyzed carefully. Because of the multiple-use nature of the resort, many requirements are placed upon it.

In addition to the parameters already mentioned, these MAIN POINTS must be considered in search of a successful site for the *RedRock Canyon Territory* PROJECT:

ONE: The AESTHETIC CHARACTER of the site is an essential part of *The Territory's* design. It is absolutely necessary for its success; a lesser substitute could result in failure of the whole project. A site that says "the Old West" cannot be compromised.

TWO: CLOSE PROXIMITY TO A LARGE POPULATION BASE (a major city or combination of cities) is also essential to its success; providing regular, repeat visitors, access to an international airport, other draws to bring in tourists, places for them to stay, and other resources.

THREE: The site must have a SUFFICIENT WATER SUPPLY for the current and projected needs of the project.

FOUR: The site must be located in a MILD SUNNY CLIMATE that won't limit the length of the tourist/filmmaking season. The park is primarily an outdoor "facility" requiring moderate temperature for both tourists and filmmakers. Because many of the sets are built of wood and plaster, a DRY ENVIRONMENT is also necessary for low maintenance. Historically, wallpaper and plaster walls could not and were not used in humid environments. Tourists will also enjoy a DRY air, even if the air temperature is high.

Secondary considerations should include the following:

FIVE: Look for virgin land with a CLASSIC WESTERN LOOK. Filmmakers (and audiences) today do not find backlots acceptable: painted backdrops, dead-end streets, nowhere for outlaws to "ride out of town". Western towns need wide expanses of western landscape visible at the ends of the streets. Audience want to see land that suggests an arid, rugged hugeness that is the American West to moviegoers. The *Classic Western Look* is as important for the tourist experience of "stepping into a Western."

SIX: Look for a site that has as many micro-landscape features as possible. Filmmakers need a VARIETY OF LANDSCAPE FEATURES to satisfy most western scripts: rivers, creeks, canyons, hills, sand dunes, forests, etc. But it is surprising how little of each can do the job over and over.

SEVEN: SOIL CONDITIONS: Choose a sight made of a soil other than a chalky white. Darker soils such as red reflects much less light, thus reducing glare and contrast for both filmmakers and tourists alike. In the site survey, note also the behavior of the soil in both dry and wet conditions. Some soils also pack down well when walked on to provide a good hard surface without the necessity of paving town streets.

EIGHT: Select a site that is OUTSIDE the EXTRA-TERRITORIAL JURISDICTION of the neighboring cities.

NINE: INCORPORATE *"The Territory"* as a city. Having jurisdiction over building codes and ordinances, water supply and sewage treatment, circumvents the limitations of using, new, creative, "non standard" building techniques, and secondly, paying for services - such as police and fire - that have to be duplicated anyway within the park.

TEN: Consider all GOVERNMENT REGULATIONS and restrictions that might result from existing site conditions, historical architecture, archaeological remains, mining operations, wildlife, etc. GET EPA APPROVAL and do impact studies well before start of construction.

In the search for an ideal site, areas that already have one or more of the man-made features or operations needed for *The Territory* will be looked at.

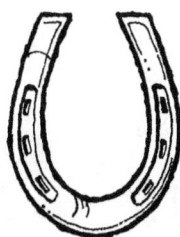

Look at WORKING CATTLE AND HORSE RANCHES with buildings, operations, and wranglers in place. A lot of expense is involved in providing cattle and horses for use in the park, making an already established working ranch an advantage. Look also at operating GUEST RANCHES.

Look at existing WESTERN MOVIE RANCHES. Though the sets on these scenic ranches are not usually built to last, they, having been "art directed" are of nice design, beautifully sited on the landscape, and can be brought up to *Territory* specks, or used as the "Ghost Town" in the proposal. The landowners are usually Western buffs and would likely be amenable to the *Red Rock Canyon* concept.

Look at LAND ADJACENT TO NATIONAL OR STATE PARKS, BLM's or National Forests. This protects one or more borders of *The Territory* from modern encroachment and gives filmmakers other locales to shoot scenes at while working in the park.

Look at OPERATING TOURIST RAILROADS run on steam, both standard and narrow-gauge lines. Running a steam railroad is an expensive operation requiring engine repair facilities, coal storage, right-of-way maintenance equipment, skilled employees, etc. which could be an asset to the project.

The **SITE SEARCH PROCEDURE** should follow this process:

Select areas of the country based on the above parameters.
Secure U.S. Geological survey maps of the sites.
Visit the most likely places and explore them.
Narrow down the options to several alternatives.
Analyze each site's natural and man-made features and the site's favorable and unfavorable aspects.

A **PRELIMINARY ENGINEERING REPORT** on each possible site should include:

A description of the area.
Topography and proposed improvements.
A land use plan.
100-year flood computations.
Existing and projected populations.
Itemized cost estimates of proposed capital improvements.
Projected tax and utility rates.
Eligibility to the National Register of Historic Places.

I'd like to finish this chapter with the following quote:

"For every site there is an ideal use. For every use there is an ideal site."
— John Ormsbee Simonds, *Landscape Architecture*, 1961

IN CONCLUSION

"Happy trails to you
Keep smiling until then
Happy trails to you
Till we meet again."
— Dale Evans (theme song from the *Roy Rogers Show,* 1951)

The western towns seen in the movies exist only on a few frames of celluloid. They're built out of paper and plaster, false fronts supported by a few braces, standing ready to fall at the first winds. The legend of the American West is forever locked into the two-dimensional world of the film strip. Until now. *RedRock Canyon Territory* is the first real "living movie" where a western fan can step into the nineteenth century and see his fantasies come to life. Stagecoaches churn up dust on a desert floor, a train whistle blows in the distance and a vulture lands on a fence post. It's the West of folklore and romance. *RedRock Canyon* is an enchanting environment of sky and earth, of western architecture and people in period costume. *RedRock Canyon* is a **reel** town, a period setting that embodies all the **spirit and flavor** of the roaring western frontier as projected on the big silver screen. *RedRock Canyon* is a **living outdoor museum** designed to inform and educate future generations about an important period in our history. It is a **tribute** to the American Western and those who created them. It is a bold new **themed resort** for western fans and the general public alike. It's also a **retirement community** for western stars. *RedRock Canyon* is a **movie ranch** where westerns can be "lensed" to perfection with a large variety of sets and all the facilities needed to do a Cinematastic job. *RedRock Canyon* provides a place to headquarter **living history groups** and organizations, providing office space, promotional services and a grand outdoor theatre to those dedicated to the preservation of the American West of history and folklore.

A TIME MACHINE

Time has come to a halt here, the pace is slower, the architecture is warm and comforting—no cold glass and steel—clear skies at night reveal bright, twinkling stars. The town marshal makes his rounds, collecting taxes and stray dogs, a store keeper loads provisions onto a farmers wagon, a cavalry Captain calls his troops out for inspection, and a cowboy bathes in a railroad water tank. The romance and nostalgia of the American West is alive and well here. The park is made to belong to the land, and the people are made to feel at home. Surrounded by hills, secluded in a valley, seemingly far from today's hectic world, **RedRock Canyon Territory** is a guaranteed success in a high stress world where we long for a peace of mind and the remembrances of our childhood.

THE WESTERN TOWN AESTHETIC

A rustic western town sitting alone on an endless desert has a timeless beauty of its own that cannot be described on paper, but must be experienced to be appreciated. The real ghost towns of the Old West are quickly disappearing—few remnants are left—it's a heritage that we must preserve for future generations who will know only large inhumane cities surrounded by miles and miles of suburbs.

PERCEPTIVE BY FEELING

Like no other theme park in the past, we want guests to respond to the park using all their senses, to cultivate the sense of the beautiful, to understand the harmony we once had with the land; living off the land with buildings made of wood and horses for transportation and living things all existing together.

In today's plastic amusement parks, people are only spectators—walking down crowded asphalt streets past a grotesque, glitzy artificiality that is engulfing our society. Brightly painted gift shops and carney games leave nothing to the imagination, no mental effort is required and guests leave the park with no enlightenment, newfound curiosity, or larger understanding of the world. In contrast, **RedRock Canyon Territory** is a living community of employees and guests who are enticed to participate and involve themselves in the total experience; to learn of a life style before electronics where ingenious mechanical solutions were the order of the day and you couldn't pick up a telephone to call for help. In **RedRock Canyon Territory** guests and employees alike will be able to sit back and enjoy the legend that is the Old West.

— **Don Kirk, 1992**

ABOUT THE AUTHOR

"It is difficult to say what is impossible, for the dream of yesterday is the hope of today and the realty of tomorrow."

— Robert H. Goddard, inventor of the rocket.

DON KIRK grew up watching westerns on a small black-and-white television set and watching western serials at Saturday morning movie matinees, but it wasn't until he was asked to be the cinematographer on an 8mm movie at college (he had the only movie camera), did he realize he was hooked on the Old West. The next year, he wrote and directed a seventy minute, silent, slapstick western in Super 8! As soon as he graduated from college with a degree in architecture, he and his brother Doug loaded provisions into a Volkswagen beetle and made their first journey West to California, shooting film all along the way. It wasn't long after that, that he conceived a plan for an Old West Resort and Western Town he originally called "Arizona Territory". Since then his interest in the American West has grown by leaps and bounds.

After a tour of duty in the Army, Don's interest in the real American West grew and he began to collect period antiques, western history books, and western costumes—anything western. He managed a Wild West gunfight acting troupe and later participated in living history reenactment groups. As time passed, he gained more than ten years experience in television commercials and motion picture production, six years of practical building experience, and years of dabbling with pen & ink artwork—his subjects, of course, were western towns and steam railroads!

Don traveled the western states for the last ten years documenting, through still photography, the rapidly disappearing remnants of a unique era in World history. Because of his interest also in architecture, he has built a veritable slide file of false-fronted Victorian buildings, wagons, schools, churches, mine complexes and any remaining architecture he could still find standing from the nineteenth century.

He has dreamed of the perfect "Western Town" for over 20 years and believes that it could be much more than a theme park. It could be a historical look into a very unique part of our past, a period that is getting farther and farther removed from the present with a loss of not only memories but the values of the people that settled the frontier and gave us what we have today. *RedRock Canyon Territory* would be the largest open-air museum ever built, it would be a unique mix of services and activity, all catering to the buff, historian and general public who want to learn and revel in the legend of our American West.

A MILL ON THE CRYSTAL RIVER IN COLORADO

PART VI: APPENDICES

REDROCK CANYON TERRITORY © DON KIRK

APPENDIX A:
Town Businesses Summary

"It's good to cherish old things. Beauty is always on the edge of being lost."

— Martin Landau, in an episode of *Outer Limits*

For a unique look at the daily life of the early west, stroll the boardwalks past the businesses of the nineteenth century. This appendix lists all of the entertainment, museums, accommodations, and restaurants discussed in this proposal.

WAGON WHEEL GAP (Cattle & Mining Center)

Street Entertainment (*Front Street Gang*)	Live entertainment: gunfight skits.
The Copper Dollar Saloon	Refreshments, live entertainment.
The Jack of Spades Gambling House	Entertainment: simulated gambling.
The Old Church	Exhibit, weddings.
Territorial Courthouse	Recreated courtroom trials.
Crazy Nell's Dance Hall & Saloon	Entertainment: music and dance.
Hook & Ladder Company No. 1 Firehall	Exhibit, live entertainment.
Merchant Wagon Shows (*Wagon Wheel Ruts*)	Live entertainment: skits.
Grand Opera House (*Stock Company Variety Players*)	Show: melodrama.
Virginia O'Donnell's Barbershop & Bathhouse	Service: haircuts and bathes.
The Carson Mansion	Entertainment: haunted house.
Wells, Fargo & Company Express Offices	Museum of the American Western.
The Nickelodeon	Theatre: early B&W western films.
Badlands Movie House	Theatre: widescreen westerns.
Electric Light Plant	Museum: Lighting history.
Guns & Gunsmithing, Nathan Wainright, Prop.	Museum: 19th-century weapons.
Johnson Land & Cattle Company Land Office	Museum of Cowboy and Western Art.
Miners Union Hall	Museum: "Truth & Legend."
Molly Fannin's Boarding House For Young Ladies	Muesum: brothel.
Museum of 19th-Century Technology	Museum: industrial revolution.
J. T. Grosenbacher General Merchandise	Exhibit: Recreated interior.
Sheriff's Office and Jail	Exhibit: furnished interior.
Clancey's Barbershop	Exhibit: furnished interior.
Doc Hanson Drugs	Exhibit: Doctor's office/drug store.
Wagon Wheel Gap Schoolhouse	Exhibit: furnished interior.
Livery, Feed & Grain	Exhibit: recreated interior.
The Wagon Yard	Exhibit: wagons.
Mortimer Peel's Undertaker & Fine Furniture	Exhibit: Mortician's office.
Nathan T. Steel, Attorney At Law	Exhibit: lawyer's office.

Copper Dollar Saloon	Refreshments.
Brass Rail Saloon	Refreshments.
Delmonico's	Food: exotic.
Bent Horseshoe Cookhouse	Food: hickory-smoked barbecue.
Penny Copperfield's Iced Cream Parlor	Food: icecream and candy.
Connie's Confectionery	Food: baked goods.
Street Venders	Food: soft drinks and snacks.
Crystal Palace Hotel	Overnight accommodations: 1880's.
Maggie Belle's Boarding House	Bed and Breakfast: 1880's.
Palace Grand Hotel	Overnight accommodations: 1880's.
Wagon Wheeel Gazette Newspaper Office	Printing: old moveable type press.
Horace Putney Photography	Photography: museum/portrait studio.
Tiny Flinn's Blacksmith Shop	Ironwork: iron puzzles for sale.
Bird's Boot & Saddle	Leatherwork: boots for sale.
Wheelright, Jesse Morales, Prop.	Woodworking: dolls & toys for sale.
Sara-Jene's Candle Shop	Candlemaking: decorative candles.
Henderson Lumber & Fencing	Lumber yard & sawmill.
Duey's Ice Plant	Manufacturing: ice.
Henley Books	Books, videotapes & laserdiscs.
Music Shop	Musical instruments, CD's & tapes.
H. B. Frank Drygoods	Reproduction period clothing.
Hennessey's Haberdashery	19th century hats & handkerchiefs.
Arthur Overstreet's Cigars	Cigar store: Pipes, tobacco & cigars.
Territorial Marshal's Office	Info.center, lost & found, first aid.
Telegraph office (at train depot)	Telegraph, and telephone services.
Pony Express Office	Post Office.
Clarence Tuttle's City Bank	Bank services, *frontier money* issued.
Other Buildings:	Doctor Leroy Sharp (Dentist),
	Chin Jung's Chinese Laundry,
	Hardware, Carlos Rodriguez, Prop.

TINCUP (Mining Camp)

Timothy McFarland's Mining Supplies	Exhibit: recreated interior.
Consolidated Mining Assay Ofice	Exhibit: Mining history, photos.
Veronica Swain's Laundry & Fortunes Told	Entertainment: fortune teller.
Potter Sweeny's Tin Shop	Gifts: pottery, tinware, graniteware.
Golden Nugget Miner's Bar	Refreshments, live entertainment.
The Grubstake Hash House	Food:"home-cooked"miner's meals.
Entertainment (*Sourdough Mining Company Players*)	Entertainment: street shows.
Mining Claims	Exhibit: headframes.
Fool's Creek Placer Mining	Entertainment: gold panning.
Murdock Gold & Silver Mining & Milling Company:	
Ore-Bucket Tram	Ride: Skyway from *Tincup*.
Murdock Mining Museum	Museum: Gold processing.
Tommyknocker Mine Tour	Ride: Underground adventure.
Dead Horse Canyon Water Flume	Exhibit: waterflume.

TinCup Train Depot   Ride: steam train.
Goldfield Overland Mail Stage Station   Ride: stagecoach.
Other Buildings: Miner's Cabins, Grist Mill, Cribs,
                                            Last Hope Saloon, Tent Residences.

DIABLO (Mexican Village)

Sangre de Cristo Spanish Mission   Exhibit: weddings.
Lost Donkey Cantina   Refreshments.
El Paso Del Norte Cafe   Food: Mexican.
Main Plaza Open-Air Market   Food, refreshments, gifts, ent.
Pedro's Stock Pens   Mule rides.
Juan Cordova's Mexican Hacienda   Bed & Breakfast: period.
Hotel Comfort   Exhibit: recreated interior.
Villa Santiago   Museum: Spanish family.
Sergio's Glass Blowing Shop   Glassblowing, gifts, stained glass.
Paco's Shoe & Leather Goods   Leathermaking: gunbelts, sandals.
Village Weaver   Weaving: basket & tapestry.
Little Wolf's Indian Goods   Gifts: pottery, blankets, jewelry, beads.
La Casa Don Antonio   Gifts: ceramics, crystal, folk art.
Estacion Diablo.   Ride: steam train.
Sweetwater Express Stage Station   Ride: stagecoach.

JACKRABBIT FLATS (Ghost Town)

Jackrabbit Flats Train Depot   Ride: steam train.
Crippled Dog Saloon   Refreshments & snacks.
Sheriff's Office & Jail   Exhibit, cobwebbed interior.
Provisions & Drygoods   Entertainment: animated interior.
Boot Hill Cemetery   Exhibit, recreated setting.
Night Life   Exhibit: Sound show.
Stage Stop   Ride: stagecoach.

FORT CARSON (Frontier Outpost)

Post Headquarters   Information & rest area.
Post Warehouse   Museum: Indian & Civil War cavalry.
Post Trader's Store   Exhibit: recreated interior, gifts.
Post Bakery   Food: baked goods.
Guardhouse   Exhibit: recreated interior.
Officer's Quarters   Museum, Victorian furnishings.
Enlisted Men's Barracks   Exhibit, recreated interior.
Enlisted Men's Bar   Refreshments, entertainment.
Quartermasters Corral and Stable   Exhibit: recreated interior.
Post Kitchen and Mess Hall   Food: Beef and Venison.
Quartermaster Supply   Gifts: Military clothing.
Other Buildings: Powder Magazine, Granary, Hospital,
                                            Blacksmith's Shop, Carpenter Shop,
                                            Laundresses Quarters, Post Cemetery.

THE BROKEN SPUR (Cattle and Horse Ranch)

Main House	Information headquarters.
Bunkhouse	Exhibit.
The Bunkhouse	Overnight accommodations.
Barn	Ride: trail rides on horseback.
Corral	Living History Demonstrations.
The Cook's Shack	Food: Barbecue.
Campfire	Live entertainment: storytelling.
Other Buildings:	Smokehouse, Milk & Meat House, Outhouse, Windmill & Water Tank.
Rodeo Arena	Show: rodeo event demonstrations.

HEAMMAWIHIO (Indian Encampment)

Indian Cave Museum	Museum: Indian artifacts.
Tribal Ceremonies	Living history demonstrations.

WESTERN RAILROAD ENTERTAINMENT

Railyard	Exhibit: railway equipment.
Buzzard's Roost Railroad Hotel	Overnight Accommodations.
Harvey House	Food: steaks & sandwiches.
Ice House	Exhibit: Wax Museum.

ENGINE HOUSE MUSEUM

Engine House	Museum: R.R. union workers.
Machine Shop	Exhibit: machining equipment.
Supply Depot	Exhibit: expendable store room.
Handcar House & Tool Shed	Exhibit: Handcar and track repair.
Watertank & Pumphouse	Exhibit: Functioning water station.
Stock Pens	Structure (exterior only).
Railroad Section House	Structure (exterior only).
The "Donegan"	Structure (exterior only).
Other Structures:	Coal Tipple & Sand House
	Watchman's Shanty
	Turntable & Roundhouse
	Tunnels & Trestles.

PARK ENTRANCE

Ticket Offices, Last Chance Gift Shop, Service Station and Auto Repair, transit services, costume rental, pet care, lockers, wheelchairs, etc.

APPENDIX B:
Park Parameters

"Western history is a field bifurcated between nostalgia and antiquarianism on the one hand (which sells) and scholarly investigation (which does not). The problem is for historians to enlarge their vision, to make the West interesting, relevant, and related to frontier experience worldwide. How can we [as historians] combine groundbreaking with an enlarged readership so necessary to success? It is a challenge to authors and editors."
— Robin Higman & Homer E. Socolofsky, "Journal of the West", 1977.

This appendix includes questions to be asked in analyzing the park's potential as a multi-use entertainment destination encompassing a museum, recreational resort, and movie production location. Parameters for each are outlined below.

GENERAL PARAMETERS

1. What values are held by the PEOPLE who will visit the park?
2. What ATTRACTIONS will the town have to offer the tourist, the filmmaker, and the western buff?
3. What FACILITIES AND SERVICES will be offered to provide the "creature comforts" of home: lodging, camping and trailer parks, food service, automobile services, and protective services such as first aid and dog kennels.
4. What TRANSPORTATION access is provided to and from the park?
5. What INFORMATION AND DIRECTION services will be provided to the tourist in advance so that he knows where he is going and what he might find if he were there?

MUSEUM PARAMETERS

1. What GROUP OF PEOPLE will be interested in American History, the Old West and western movies? Western film buffs, 'Old West' fans, historians, general public? What age groups?
2. Will the park have sufficient AUTHENTICITY to attract serious buffs and historians?

3. Will the park be EDUCATIONAL?
4. Do the period towns within the park have a LOGICAL REASON FOR EXISTENCE designed into them? Are they railheads, mining camps, railroad junctions, land promotions, the capitol city, a trail crossroads, watering hole?
5. What is the parks TIME AND LOCATION in history? Do all the elements - props, antiques, set dressing, technology, transportation, and building materials - belong to a specific time and place? Telephone or telegraph, steam-driven vehicle or horse-drawn wagon, hand-forged window glass or manufactured panes?
6. How does the PHYSICAL SETTING affect a) the towns reason for existence, b) the architecture of the town and c) the general character and layout of the town.
7. What BUSINESSES would be typically found in these towns and what SOCIAL ACTIVITIES would typically occur?

RECREATIONAL PARK PARAMETERS

1. Is there easy access to the site by busses, automobiles and campers?
2. Is there sufficient overnight accommodation?
3. Is the site along tourist routes and not at the end of a long dead-end route?
4. Are there other tourist draws in the area to make it a destination point and thus keep the tourist for several days.
5. Are there activities within the park for all age groups?
6. Are walking distances within the park kept to a minimum so as to not exhaust and "wear out" the guest?
7. Are first aid, child care and dog kennels available?
8. Is the live entertainment, rides and amusements appropriate to the park; and are they what the guests would expect to find at that type of facility?
9. Is the quality of experience at the park sufficiently superior to expectations that the guests will leave the park pleased.
10. Shopping is always a major objective of tourists. Are there sufficient things of interest to purchase?
11. Will the park provide pleasure, fun, excitement, awe AND educational values?
12. Is there a good separation of the "fantasy world" of the park from the extraneous visuals and noise of the 'outside world' such as airplanes, city noise, automobiles, utility power lines, weather, etc.?
13. Does the park provide ample photographic opportunities for the instant camera user AND the more serious photographer? (The pictures guests take is a major word-of-mouth advertising tool—so the better their pictures the more guests there will be in the future.)

14. Does the ownership and management of the park care about the quality of the product they are putting out. Do they have a passion for the subject matter, do they care about the employees that work for them. Is profit the owner's only objective?

MOVIE RANCH PARAMETERS

A film "location" away from Hollywood has to meet certain minimum conditions to satisfy the requirements of a film production company. Questions asked by a movie company about the location would include the following:

1. Can a crew of 100 or so be accommodated?
2. Is there local "help" available to work on the film (production assistants, location people, etc.)?
3. What labor is available locally, for carpentry, craft work, etc?
4. Can the production company get the needed extras locally?
5. What are the roads like to and from the location?
6. Will the weather be good at this time of year?
7. How much variety in "sets" and locations can be achieved at this one site?
8. What buildings on site can double as housing for film crews?
9. What is the travel time from the airport?
10. How far is it to additional movie company support facilities, such as hotels, restaurants, grip, lighting and camera rental houses, post production facilities, etc?
11. Exactly what facilities are offered and at what price?
12. What is the ambient noise level from surrounding city and traffic?
13. What accommodations are available on the site and outside the park?
14. Is there a theatre with an interlock projection system for showing dailies?
15. How close is the nearest processing lab?
16. Is there sufficient electrical power to supply the lighting needs of a production company?
17. Are there production offices to work out of?
18. What props and set dressing is available on site?
19. Can each western town set appear as several different towns?
20. Are there other "out buildings" beyond the town proper available for use as sets?
21. Is there expansion space to allow production companies to build additional needed sets?
22. Is a sound stage available for building interior sets?
23. Are there any "practical sets" in the buildings for interior shooting?

24. Are horse stables and corrals available for care and feeding of animals brought in for filming?
25. What kind of backgrounds are visible beyond the town?
26. What surrounding terrain can be used as sets?
27. What other resources are available to support the needs of a film production company?

APPENDIX M1:
Marketing Strategy

"The resurgence of Westerns in movies and on TV stems from the fact people yearn for a simpler time. I think we long for an age without technology. That's what Westerns give us."
— Christian Clemenson, co-star of *Adventures of Brisco County Jr.*, 1993

This appendix lists some of the selling approaches that *RedRock Canyon Territory* will focus on in its marketing strategy. The use of the right WORDS, and VISUALS are key to their success. Following this section are sample marketing publications: a guest information brochure, "Sunday magazine" story, radio ad, and spinoff projects to promote the park.

There are now over 170 living history sites in operation around the U.S. In 1992, 15 percent of all adults in the U.S. visited a theme park. One-third of Americans believe they don't have enough time to spend with their families, and a solid majority of Americans (61%) would be willing to take a salary cut if it resulted in an increase in there free time.

These statistics suggest that entertainment that is perceived to be more WORTH WHILE will have an edge over "pure entertainment", adding VALUE to the customer's time. They want leisure that has some meaning.

RedRock Canyon Territory could also provide a RELIEF TO THE SENSORY OVERLOAD that Americans are experiencing today, what with the television blasting electronic images of world events at a dizzying pace, daily traffic snarls, the drone of traffic, the shriek of sirens; car alarms, beepers and cell phones going off, the feeling that there is no way to escape. Even a "vacation" to a theme park reveals the same atmosphere: masses of people, lines, confusion, color, metal & plastic, high noise—a bombardment of electrons.

RedRock Canyon Territory will promote itself as an ALTERNATIVE way to spend the customer's valuable vacation time. An escape from today's reality to a time remembered.

RedRock Canyon Territory will promote the park as an open-air museum where one can learn and experience new things. Museums have perpetually had to deal with the "stodgy" image and boring presentation of shelved artifacts and written information. As a possible solution, *The Territory* presents history in an INTERESTING and ENTERTAINING way, a living history that can be INTERACTED with.

People are searching for VALUES to return to in this world of violent crime and big government. A return to the perceived wholesome values that the American frontier represent—Individualism, honesty, honor, self-reliance, etc. Parents want to take their kids to a place that is ALSO perceived to have wholesome "Gunsmoke" values; those the "baby-boomers" were raised on.

People are looking for a QUIET, BACK-TO-NATURE place to escape to. Look at the attendance at National and State parks, and guest ranches. *RedRock Canyon* can offer so much more!

Many INTERNATIONAL TRAVELERS come to the United States looking for the West they've seen in the movies, but they usually don't find it because it requires the renting of a car and driving thousands of miles around the West. *RedRock Canyon Territory* would allow them to fly to a single location and experience the West of their FANTASIES. (Footnote: TEXAS is the only state most foreigners can name, a promotional asset if the park is done in Texas. "Texas: Where The Wild West Was Invented.")

The West is a symbol of PIONEERING EXPERIENCE all over the world. To them its ROMANTIC. The JAPANESE admire it. They come to the U.S. to find it: A classless society where everyone is equal (not so in Japan).

The Territory has some similarities to the theme park presented in the movie "Westworld", where the experience is INTERACTIVE. Guests are participants. The experience becomes part of them and thus more memorable. *The Territory* is a "come and stay awhile" experience rather than "go and see it".

RedRock Canyon Territory is a COMMUNITY. A confluence of people and ideas related to the American West. The employees who work in this park are made up of people who represent many interests and disciplines, but have in common, a passion for the "American West": historians, re-enactors, railroad fans, Old West buffs, architects, historic preservationists, western movie actors, country & western singers, cowboy poets, etc. *The Territory* could become the "Jerusalem" of the "Western religion".

Guests who come to *The Territory* will FIND THE GOLD. Promotions will play on the ROMANTICISM and NOSTALGIA of the Old West.

"Share the spirit, adventure, and Romance of the West." "Come where you can once again get a 50-cent Saturday-night haircut and bath." "RedRock Canyon: Where Anyone Can Be A Westerner."

Visitors who come to *RedRock Canyon Territory* will "see the elephant", a phrase that symbolized for the 49er gold rushers "the exotic, the mythical, the once-in-a-lifetime adventure, of a journey to the promised land of fortune: California." Now we can substitute *"RedRock Canyon"*. for "California".

Market segments will be targeted, taking advantage of the magazines and publications purchased by those segments.

RedRock Canyon Territory is FAMILY FRIENDLY—fun for the whole family—something they can do together—to talk about. Promote the MUSEUM nature of the park; it's educational values. The public will perceive *The Territory* as MORE WORTHWHILE than many other parks. Children can see history re-created, ride a stagecoach, drink sarsaparilla and ride an "onry" mule.

To avoid scaring off a large family looking at expensive, per person, all day, all-inclusive tickets, R.R.C.T. will try to offer a large range of ticketing options: riding only the train, staying only part of the day, seeing specific shows without paying the entire day entrance fee, family group rates, etc.

RedRock Canyon will promote the AUTHENTICITY of *The Territory* as a source for new understanding of life in the Old West. The architecture, the food, and the entertainment won't just be descriptions in a textbook.

FOLKWAYS AND PIONEER CRAFTS, including building crafts, are preserved and perpetuated at the park, bringing together the older generations of Americans who want to pass on these almost lost arts. There are Associations for almost every old-world craft whose members would enjoy such a place as *RedRock Canyon Territory*.

RE-ENACTORS and LIVING HISTORIANS will be targeted with an offer of camaraderie and networking with others around the world with similar interests. *RedRock Canyon* would provide a place to re-create battles and historical events, and it would have the largest collection in one place of period clothing and accoutrements available for sale. And don't forget the large library of western literature for doing research.

WESTERN MOVIE BUFFS can come to meet western movie stars, see their favorite western movie once again on the big screen, buy movie memorabilia, and see museum collections that pay tribute to western actors, directors and western movie locations.

RedRock Canyon Territory will establish a NON PROFIT ASSOCIATION to draw "fans" together and promote the park. It would provide information about the park, publications, a calendar of events, and contests with a prize of a free trip to *The Territory*. The Association could also provide a vehicle for raising large donations to the park. The organization might be called the "Association for the Preservation and Enjoyment of the American West of Fact and Legend"!

Stamp Mill, Idaho Springs, Colorado

APPENDIX M2:
Guest Information Brochure

"Out where the West begins, out where the handclasp's a little stronger, out where the smile dwells a little longer; that's where the West begins."

—Arthur Chapman

The assignment: an information brochure to be sent to prospective guests and tour groups outlining the facilities and services available at the park. Written by Don Kirk.

RedRock Canyon Territory
GUEST INFORMATION

DESCRIPTION. *RedRock Canyon Territory* is the largest open-air museum in the world—authentically recreating the American West in the 1870's. Several period towns, and a ranch and military fort, are accessed by horse-drawn stagecoaches and a narrow gauge, steam-driven train. The railroad is a time machine, that will take you back into another era.

FEATURES. *The Territory* is populated with people in period costume, representing Old West characters in all walks of life: townspeople, farmers, ranchhands and miners. Period activities of all kinds are meticulously re-created, from Fourth-of-July picnics to medicine wagon shows, opera house plays and cavalry drills. Numerous exhibits re-create 19th-century shops like the general store and barbershop. There are movie houses that pay tribute to the Western movie and museums displaying the weapons, art and photography of the period. Living historians teach the history, folklore, traditions, customs, and crafts of the immigrants who settled the West. 19th-century materials and techniques are used to authentically recreate the architecture of the period. Even the meals are designed from authentic recipes and served in restaurants with a period decor. Various businesses in the park sell hand-made crafts, gifts and clothing—any and everything related to the western movie and the American West of fact and legend.

LOCATION. *RedRock Canyon Territory* is in an arid, cactus-strewn valley surrounded by hills and rock outcroppings, secluded from today's modern world so that the illusion of actually being in the American West of the 19th century will not be destroyed by modern sights and sounds.

HOURS. The park is open year around, seven days a week, from dawn to midnight. Spring and fall is the most popular and comfortable time to visit the park. Even during bad weather, the park is an adventure, dust blowing through the streets, rain running through gullies and dripping off the porch roofs.

ADMISSIONS. Several ticket options are provided for your convenience. DAY PASSES for individuals include general admission and train ticket to the valley, unlimited transportation within *The Territory* and most live entertainment. For those travelers reaching the park late in the day, they can purchase general admission tickets for that evening AND the next day OR half-day passes for the evening only. Special discounted "RETURN PASSES" are available to those guests who, upon leaving the park, decide they want to come back the next day. FAMILY PASSES provide discounted package prices for your family or group for a stay of several days. TOUR GROUP RATES for organizations and international travelers of 25 or more are sold in advance and must be pre-paid at least two weeks in advance.

FRONTIER CURRENCY. Your 1990's dollars can be converted to *Frontier Money* (at pre-inflation prices) to be used for food, gifts and entertainment within the park (a haircut and straight-razor shave can be had for 25 cents in *Frontier Money*!)

ACCOMMODATIONS. There are several hotels within *The Territory* proper that authentically recreate nineteenth-century accommodations with the beauty of old period furnishings, natural ventilation and bathrooms down the hall! These hotel rooms are for the hardy souls who can't get enough of the Old West during the day. Units are limited, so reservations well ahead of your visit are recommended. But you softies, don't fret: modern hotels at the perimeter of the park have ALL the conveniences you need for a relaxing stay in the American West of the 20th century!

PARKING. There is plenty of auto and motorcoach parking at the "jumping off point" where you will board a steam train that takes you into colorful **Red Rock Canyon**.

FOOD. Several period restaurants within *The Territory* serve authentic food prepared from historically accurate recipes of that era. Old-fashioned

meals with a southwest flavor, Mexican border dishes, smoked and barbecued "cowboy ranch" meals, down-home miner's and cavalry "grub", and "eastern hotel" cuisine prepared in the finest traditions of the American West, provide a variety of tasty but authentic meals for all pallets. In *The Territory*, you'll also find numerous period food carts serving snacks, beverages and ice-cream. Water is available throughout the park. YOU MAY NOT BRING FOOD AND DRINK INTO THE TERRITORY. Reserved or prearranged seating or menu selection is not available. Catering is available for prearranged evening events and private parties.

LENGTH OF STAY. Because there are so many activities (live entertainment, museums, craft shops, furnished interiors, restaurants and architecture) to experience in *The Territory*, several days are recommended for full enjoyment of the park. And because it is a full service resort with "guest ranch activities" like cookouts, horseback riding, swimming, tennis, and Old West research facilities, **RedRock Canyon Territory** can easily become your sole destination for a relaxing, adventure-packed vacation. But if you are limited to just one day, you can get a good overview of the park by visiting the largest town sets and exploring some of the museums. There are many evening activities and special shows you can "take-in".

DRESS. We suggest that you dress casually and wear comfortable shoes. Streets are not paved; expect dust and even mud when it rains. There will be a lot of walking, but transportation in the form of a horse-drawn stagecoach service and a steam railroad is provided to get you to the various town centers and villages within the park. Special transportation is provided for the aged and handicapped to get them around the park. Guests are encouraged to come dressed as westerners with at least a hat to protect them from the sun, and some costuming is available for daily rental at the park entrance. CAMERAS ARE WELCOME. Camcorder holsters and over-the-shoulder "possibles" bags are available for hiding your camera and video equipment so they will fit in with your "outfit".

FIRST AID. First Aid is available in *The Territory* at each of the three "towns" and at the fort and cattle ranch.

ANIMALS. Sorry, pets are not allowed in *The Territory* (we have enough of our own to tend to). But kennels are available at the park entrance.

GENERAL INFORMATION

For your convenience, at the park entrance you will be given a guide to *The Territory* that will show you how to get around and what there is to see and do. Included are territorial and town maps locating all the museums, exhibits, restaurants, shops, restrooms, and information & assistance services. The guide also provides historical information on the architecture, entertainment, crafts, foods, and living history activities you'll see in the park.

U. S. Postal mail service is available in the park, along with basic banking services (credit card advances, traveler's checks cashed, etc.) and there is communication by telegraph to each of the railroad depots around the park.

Special events tickets can be purchased for special performances, holiday celebrations and historical battle reenactments. Plan your trip to include one of these great holiday events listed in the enclosed brochure.

You may leave and return to *RedRock Canyon Territory* on the same day or over several days by picking up a special token upon your initial departure.

Individuals with disabilities are accommodated at the park. Special transportation and care facilities are provided. Call 555-1267 for further information.

Educational tour packages for school children are available for exploring the park.

If you have questions that we have not answered, please do not hesitate to contact our GUEST RELATIONS office at 1-210-646-0227. We will make every effort to insure that your visit to this historical open-air park is enjoyable, educational and entertaining. Join us for a unique and memorable experience in the Old West Territory known as *RedRock Canyon*.

(Operating times, policies and procedures are subject to change without notice.)

APPENDIX M3:
A Magazine Story

"If you build it, they will come."
— James Earl Jones, *Field Of Dreams*, 1989

The assignment: an ad in the style of a human interest story: an interview with Don Kirk (creator of **RedRock Canyon Territory**), for use in a newspaper's Sunday magazine. Written by Douglas Walter Kirk.

BRINGING THE WEST ALIVE:
TEXAS STYLE

By Douglas Kirk

One hundred years ago when you could smell the dust as it blew down Main Street in a little town on the edge of nowhere, you would have expected to see a man with a full beard amble up to a counter, punch keys on an old brass cash register and say, "that'll be two cents pardner." But not today. Today you're lucky to get a store clerk's attention at all and two cents won't buy anything, much less a sack of sugar. The only thing you can smell is automobile exhaust and street smog.

But there are people coming to Texas looking for that man with the beard, and the sound of horses pulling a wagon to a stop out in front of the General Store. There are people coming from all over the world, in fact, in search of the Old West. They're looking for the West they've seen in Hollywood movies and read about in Louis L'Amour novels. They're searching for that pioneering spirit that they know carved America out of a wilderness, that spirit that has lead man to explore the world and the heavens and beyond. But they're not finding it. "They don't find it because it's not here anymore," says the man who may just be the one to put them in touch with that dream.

"I know, I've looked for it and it's not here anymore. I've traveled all the western states—Arizona, New Mexico, Montana—and except for a few tales about Billy the Kid and some steam trains running in the mountains of Colorado, the Old West is gone. "And that's too bad, because the values of the Old West are the ideals that made this nation what it is. There was a day in Texas when you could ride into town, take care of business, and nobody would ask where you were from, where you were going or even your name. "Today they want nine credit cards, a birth certificate and three sworn affidavits, and that's just to buy a hamburger."

Don Kirk is exaggerating, of course, but the point is well taken. The spirit has changed in America and there are an awful lot of people wishing it hadn't. Don Kirk is different. He's not the type of man who wishes for things. He's the kind of man who makes them happen. One look at his house and you know that's true. It's not really correct to call it a house. Oh, he lives there, but it's more of a museum than anything else. And if you haven't been to a western museum lately, you're missing something. His old brass cash register has real gold coins in it, and paper money that dates back to the Civil War. The old confectioner's tins in the kitchen are real too, as are the cameras that were built before the turn of the century.

Every nook in his house has another story and another artifact, not piled up like so much junk, but displayed with pride behind glass like you'd see in the Smithsonian. And there isn't an inch of wall space or a foot of floor space either. The collection has long since burst its seams, with new pieces being added almost daily.

So what would prompt someone to collect such a menagerie of this and that, of things most people never knew existed?

You have to wander farther into the home to discover the real reason for the collection. You have to pass down the long hallway, through a room full of movie books and posters and film cans and cameras and stacks of western art. You have to make your way to the office, the one on the left, not the one on the right, that's the one for paying bills. Go into the one on the left, where dreams are turned into reality. If *Walt Disney* were alive, he'd be at home in a place like this, he'd be there in the dream room, there with Don Kirk working out the ideas of what has so far been a twenty year passion.

There, on a drafting table and scattered around the room, are blueprints and pictures and plans and what some people might describe as an enormous stack of scratch pads and notes. There, amidst everything else, is *The Territory*.

In South Dakota a man is trying to carve *Chief Crazy Horse* into the side of the mountain beside the Presidents of **Mt. Rushmore**. In Florida, scientists are building rockets that fly into space. But in Texas, in Texas, mind you, the only state in the Union that has as part of its constitution that it has the right to break into six other states or leave the United States altogether, in Texas, home of the Alamo, in Texas where in 1836 independence was won by a rag-tag force of patriots who overcame the entire fighting force of the nation of Mexico, in Texas there's Don Kirk and *The Territory*.

The Territory? Everybody who's anybody in the San Antonio motion picture business knows about it. It's been under wraps for 20 years, but they know about it and they've heard about it and lot of them have given advice about it. After all, it's **The Territory**. It's the all-consuming result of a man's life's work. It's the creative answer to the search that is on for the spirit and the mind and the true-life experience of the Old West culture that is famous the world over.

In some parts of the world, Texas is bigger than life and like the faithful returning to the origins of their religious beliefs for a renewal of spiritual vows, people from all over creation are traveling to Texas in search of that spirit that makes man unique on this planet.

Freedom, opportunity, equality - these are the values that made the Old West what it was and what it continues to be in the minds and hearts of men everywhere.

And this is the basis of *The Territory.* For a time, for perhaps just a few days, or a few hours, wouldn't it be something if there was a place where you could go, a place where you could step through a time portal and be transported back a hundred years and live those times and values and that spirit that is the essence of the Old West?

Twenty years in the making, thousands of photographs, diagrams, sketches, blue prints - uncounted hours of hard work and creative brilliance - that's what *RedRock Canyon Territory* is all about. It's an **Old West Resort** like the world has never known, an open-air living history museum where guests don western clothing and step into the sights and sounds and the smell of days gone by. Lost in a more simple time, where newspapers are set by hand with lead type, and where there are no telephones or microwaves and the day's events are on a human scale, some people actually refuse to come out, to go home, to return to a modern world.

"That's what I'm after", says Don Kirk, who won't say where he's been or ask you your name for fear of offending you. "It's the Code of the West, and it served the people who lived and survived in this country long before we had fast food or dime-a-dozen politicians, or income tax."

— Douglas Kirk,
freelance writer, 1993.

Rancho Alegre, Santa Fe, New Mexico

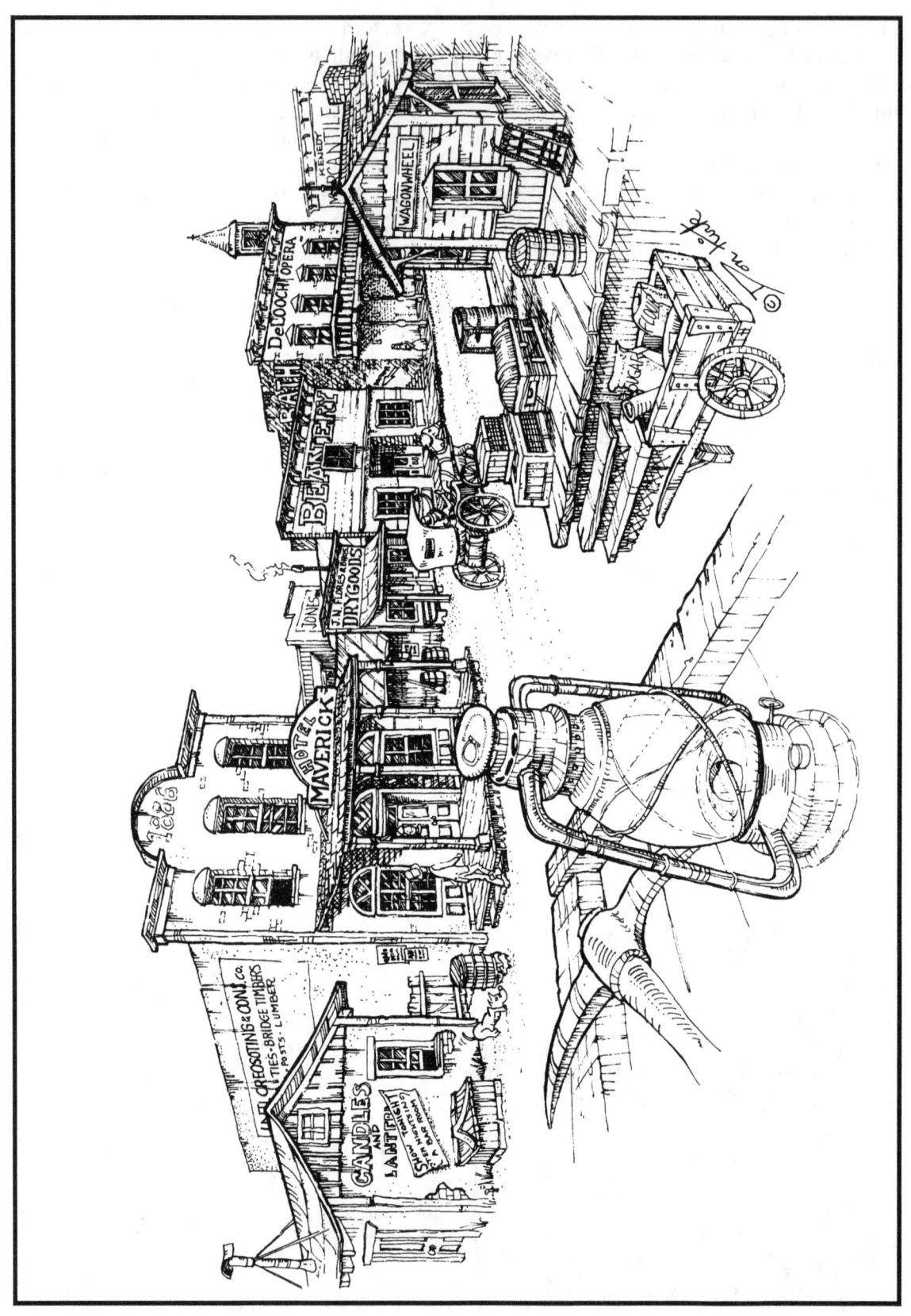

TOWNS GREW UP ALONG THE RAILROAD

APPENDIX M4:
A Radio Ad

"I've always wanted to see the frontier - before it's gone."
— Kevin Costner, *Dances with Wolves, 1990*

The assignment: a "PROSPECTOR SERIES" of RADIO SPOTS to promote **RedRock Canyon Territory**. An old prospector talks about *The Territory* and why it's worth a visit. Written by Pleasant McNeel.

VERSION ONE: "FIND THE GOLD": 30 SECONDS

The spot opens with the sounds of clopping horses hooves, rattling chains from wagon teams, children playing—the sounds of a busy 19th-century western town. Over this comes the rough, aged, and experienced voice of a gold prospector:

"Hea - hea (a chuckle)
HOWDY, this is the Old Timer—I'm sittin' here in **RedRock Canyon**—And you know, I've been prospecting these hills all my life for something valuable. I thought it was GOLD, but it ain't. Not hardly. I found what's really worthwhile, in **RedRock Canyon**!: it's true American values. It's back when you knew right from wrong—when a handshake meant something—when the words HONOR and DECENCY were not snickered at by phony people in funny looking suits. Yes, sir, GOLD! **RedRock Canyon:** a place where man can kickback with his family and find out how America used to be—or at least how it shoulda' been! He- he (a snicker)."

VERSION TWO: "FAMILY VALUES", 60 SECONDS

"Oh-he (a chuckle).
This is the Old Timer here, and I been looking around for a place I kin show my grand kids what the world was like in my day when I was a youngster. You know, kids imaginations these days are powered up by robots, and creatures from outer space—not by hard workin' men and women fightin' to settle the frontier—not heroes you can depend on—not men whose word is his bond. No sir! Here in **RedRock Canyon** you can find all those things and you can share them with your family. I know when I start a talkin' about it, I kin see their eyes roll up over.

When I use words like honor and decency, talk about a man's handshake and his word, when a man took responsibility for what he done—I see 'em looking funny and sayin': 'Ah, grampa', but out here in **RedRock Canyon**, by hoot, I kin show 'em, yes sir!—and you can bring YOUR FAMILY down here and show 'em too.'"

END

VERSION THREE: "GET-A-WAY": 30 SECONDS

The SOUND of a slight dessert breeze is heard with the squawk of an eagle echoing off canyon walls.

"Oh-he (a chuckle).
This here's the Old Timer - and you know sumpin'—it's been—goodness—I can't tell you how long since I saw television, and by golly, I don't miss it. No sir! What with violence in the streets, countries in civil war, and presidents you wouldn't buy a wagon from—it sounds to me like the world out there is goin' to the buzzards! But here at **RedRock Canyon**, things are like, well, if not like they were, at least like they shoulda been: peaceful and quiet. Why, you kin hear the cactus grow! And smell clean air. By God, for a spell you can come here an' forget your troubles and all the world's troubles, and get back into the world we wished it was: **RedRock Canyon Territory**."

The squawk of an eagle is HEARD in a wide-open space.

END

A quiet, arid land around Acoma Pueblo, New Mexico

APPENDIX M5:
Spinoffs

"An Easterner who walked into a western saloon was amazed to see a dog sitting at a table playing poker with three men. 'Can that dog really read cards?' he asked. 'Yeah, but he ain't much of a player', said one of the men, 'Whenever he gets a good hand he wags his tail.'"

— Anonymous

Fun, publicity, and profit are objectives of the businesses and merchandising "spinoffs" of *RedRock Canyon Territory*. They would each become profit centers in their own right and at the same time provide continuous PUBLICITY for the park, keeping the name before the public.

RedRock Canyon Territory: **THE VIDEO GAME.** A CD-ROM, INTERACTIVE, three dimensional video game, where the player or players can role play any western character they want in *The Territory*. The "video town" would be peopled with outlaws, lawmen and law-abiding citizens. Based on the parks design and layout, the game allows players to walk (and ride) through the territory and interact with the characters—characters who evolve and change with each new encounter.

RedRock Canyon Territory: **WESTERN GIFT STORE.** A selection of quality "Old West gift items": artwork, greeting cards, sculpture, books, memorabilia, etc. will be sold in retail outlets placed in popular tourist malls in major cities around the country. Gifts would also be sold by mail order.

The **OLD WEST CABLE CHANNEL:** Old Western movies, of course, but also interviews with western stars, behind-the-scenes looks at the making of westerns, series' about historical events, live specials covering related events like a Cowboy Poets Gathering, interviews with art directors and the musicians who write the scores, a cowboy memorabilia collectors shopping program, a regular "Events in *The Territory*" program, and so forth. The live shows would originate from the TV studio at the park making "drop-ins" easy.

The **AMERICAN WEST PUBLISHING COMPANY:** publishing original works and reprints on western subjects. The company would also publish paper goods for the gift shops: greeting cards, coloring books, card games, board games, video programs, wanted posters and broadsides. These goods would be designed around the park and use the resources of the park.

A **WESTERN MOVIE TRIVIA GAME SHOW:** A thirty-minute taped program where contestants are challenged with quotations, stills, video clips, and questions from the "Oaters". Western stars are sometimes guests, riding horseback onto the set; "shenanigans" being part of this "horse opera"!

An **OLD WEST CLOTHING STORE** for men and woman: Not "dime-store cowboy" clothing, but reproductions with authentic cuts and detailing, improved only where necessary for today's comfort. Several new mail order companies have been started in the last few years suggesting a renewed interest in this kind of line. The retail outlets would be designed with a western look and also sell clothing accoutrements: hats, neckties, pocket watches, leather goods, a saddle or two, some western memorabilia, etc.

The **VAUDEVILLE VARIETY THEATRE AND GAMBLING SALOON.** A turn-of-the-century opera house design with balconies around a central floor with a raised wooden stage at one end. Footlights, chandeliers and flocked wall paper complete the impression. Round wooden tables populate the floors instead of seating: It's a place to eat, but it's not a dinner theatre in the usual sense because tourists can come in off the street at any time, and eat a light lunch or have a drink, with vaudeville type performances at unscheduled times: stand-up comedians, ventriloquists, jugglers, magicians, melodrama plays, etc. The concept is intended for a tourist destination area. Troupes from *RedRock Canyon Territory* would tour these theatres at the end of their park run. The Gambling Room would be "token for prizes" on historically designed tables to create the Old West atmosphere.

Each of these "spinoffs" can't help but improve the profitability of *The Territory*; working in tandem to draw more guests to the park. *Walt Disney CO.*'s success with similar promotions will attest to that fact. Remember the "Disneyland" television show used to promote the Anaheim park!

APPENDIX T1:
Historical Western Films

"When in doubt, make a western."
— John Ford

Listed below are some of the "oaters" that have become historically important. Film critics will argue which films should be on the list so don't take this list as the final say. Included with the title are its director, date made, and its historical importance.

STAGECOACH, John Ford, 1939.
Rescued the genre from its dead-end decline of the 1930's, helped bring John Waye to stardom.

SHANE, George Stevens, 1953.
This film is a conscious retelling of the purest elements of the classic western legend. It codified the essence of the western.

THE SEARCHERS, John Ford, 1956.
A masterpiece pictorically. Ford's first widescreen film and considered by many to be Ford's masterpiece.

FISTFULL OF DOLLARS, Sergio Leone, 1964.
The first Italian "spaghetti western" defining a new brutal West with grittiness, offhand violence, extreme closeups and Ennio Moricone's 'jangly' soundtrack. It made Clint Eastwood a star with his "Man With No Name" character.

THE WILD BUNCH, Sam Peckinpah, 1969.
Brought the element of graphic violence to the screen with his slow-motion bloodletting. Considered to be Peckinpah's greatest film.

BUTCH CASSIDY AND THE SUNDANCE KID, George Roy Hill, 1969.
Successfully combined action with comedy. It won Burt Bacharach and Hal David an oscar for best score.

DANCES WITH WOLVES, Kevin Costner, 1990.
Reestablished the western's viability at the box Office. It won "Best Picture" and six other oscars.

UNFORGIVEN, Clint Eastwood, 1992.
A dark Western with an anti-hero; good and evil is no longer black and white. Revitalized the western as a pertinent genre. Won "Best Picture" and "Best Director" oscars.

APPENDIX T2:
Western Movie Directors

"Westerns are closer to art than anything else in the motion picture business."
— John Wayne

Some western movie directors have become as famous as the outlaws portrayed in their movies. Listed below are some of the directors that were western movie poliferate, and includes some of their best known Western films.

JOHN FORD, known for his use of Monument Valley and for making John Wayne famous. His Western films include: *Stagecoach* (1939), *My Darling Clementine* (1946), *She Wore a Yellow Ribbon* (1949), *Wagon Master* (1950), *The Searchers* (1956), *The Horse Soldiers* (1959), *The Man Who Shot Liberty Valance* (1962) and other successful westerns: *How The West Was Won* (1963), *Rio Grande* (1950), *Straight Shooting* (1917), *The Three Godfathers* (1949), *Two Ride Together* (1961) and *Cheyenne Autumn* (1964).

SAM PECKINPAH, known for his slow-motion bloody violence. Westerns films included *Ride The High Country* (1962),*Wild Bunch* (1969), *The Ballad of Cable Hogue* (1970), and *Pat Garrett and Billy The Kid* (1973). Less successful films: *Major Dundee* (1965) and *Junior Bonner* (1972).

SERGIO LEONE, created the "spaghetti western" sub-genre with a new brutal West and extreme closeups, and made Clint Eastwood a star. *Films: Fistful Of Dollars* (1964), *For a Few Dollars More* (1965), *The Good, The Bad And The Ugly* (1966), *Once Upon a Time In The West* (1969) and *A Fistful of Dynamite* (1972).

HOWARD HAWKS films: *Red River* (1948), *Rio Bravo* (1959), *El Dorado* (1967), and lesser films: *The Barbary Coast, The Outlaws* (1943) *Rio Lobo (1970)* and *The Big Sky*.

JOHN STURGES his best westerns: *Bad Day At Black Rock* (1955), *Gunfight At The O.K. Corral* (1957), *The Magnificent Seven* (1960). Others: *Last Train From Gun Hill* (1959), *The Hallelujah Trail (1965), The Law And Jake Wade* (1958) and *Joe Kidd* (1972).

DELMAR DAVES films: *The Covered Wagon* (1923), *Broken Arrow* (1950), *3.10 To Yuma* (1957) and *The Hanging Tree, The Badlanders* (1958) and *Drum Beat* (1954).

ANTHONY MANN films: *Winchester '73* (1950), The Naked Spur (1953), *The Man From Laramie* (1955), and *Man Of The West* (1958) Others: *The Tin Star* (1957) and *Bend Of The River* (1952).

BUDD BOETTICHER films: *The Man From The Alamo* (1953), *The Tall T* (1957), *Decision At Sundown* (1957), *Buchanan Rides Alone* (1958), *Ride Lonesome* (1959) and *Comanche Station* (1960).

HENRY HATHAWAY films: *North To Alaska (1960), True Grit (1969), To The Last Man* (1933), *How The West Was Won* (1963), *Nevada Smith* (1966), *Rawhide* (1951), *The Sons of Katie Elder* (1965), *From Hell To Texas* (1958), and *Five Card Stud* (1968).

BURT KENNEDY films: *Support your Local Sheriff* (1969), *The Westerner* (1940), *The Big Country* (1958), *The War Wagon* (1967), *Texas Guns* (1988), and less sucessful films: *Hannie Caulder* (1972), *Return Of The Seven* (1966), *Train Robbers* (1973) and *The Wild Wild West Revisited* TV movie (1979).

HENRY KING films: *The Gunfighter* (1950), *Jesse James* (1939) and *The Bravados* (1958).

WILLIAM WITNEY films: *The Adventures of Red Ryder* serial (1940), *Zorro Rides Again* serial (1937), *In Old Amarilo* (1951), and *Helldorado* (1946).

ROBERT N. BRADBURY made many "B" westerns, many with John Wayne: *West of the Divide* (1934), *Riders of Destiny* (1933), *The Star Packer* (1934), *Trouble in Texas* (1937), *Texas Terror* (1935) and*The Trail Beyond* (1934).

LESLEY SELANDER films: *Three Men From Texas* (1940), one of the best Hopalong Cassidy films ever made, *The Rustlers* (1949), *Buckskin Frontier* (1943), *Guns of Hate* (1948), *Brothers in the Saddle* (1949), *Rider from Tucson* (1950), *Road Agent* (1952), and dozens more.

HOWARD BRETHERTON films: *Riders of the Rio Grande* (1943), *Carson City Cyclone* (1943), *Ghost Town Law* (1942), *Hidden Valley Outlaws* (1944), *San Antonio Kid* (1944) and *West of the Law* (1942).

RAOUL WALSH films: *Dark Command* (1940), *They Died With Their Boots On* (1941), *The Big Trail* (1930) and *Gun Fury* (1953).

GEORGE SHERMAN films: *Colorado Sunset* (1939), *Kansas Cyclone* (1941), *Mexicali Rose* (1939), *Riders of the Black Hills* (1938), *Rocky Mountain Rangers* (1940), *Tulsa Kid* (1940), *Under Texas Skies* (1940).

OTHER PROLIFERATE WESTERN MOVIE DIRECTORS:

George Archainbaud	Spencer Gordon Bennet	John English
William Wyler	Joseph Kane	D. Ross Lederman
George Marshal	Sam Newfield	Andrew McLaglen
Nicholas Ray		

APPENDIX T3:
Western Stars

"I play John Wayne in every picture regardless of the character."
— John Wayne

RedRockCanyon Territory is a tribute to the American Western and the crews that made them, and that includes the actors and actresses who made so many westerns that they became forever associated with the genre.

"A" WESTERN SUPERSTARS
(They shaped our image of the Western hero.)
Tom Mix
Gary Cooper
John Wayne
Joel McCrea
Randolph Scott
Clint Eastwood

"B" WESTERN STARS
Gene Autry
Roy Rogers
Bronco Billy Anderson
Fred Thompson
Ken Maynard
Buck Jones
Tim McCoy
William Boyd
Tex Ritter

POPULAR STARS
(Popular stars that appeared successfully in Westerns. Even though they were not regarded as Western stars, they were cast in numerous Westerns.)
James Stewart
Glenn Ford
Henry Fonda
Charles Bronson
Robert Young
Yul Brynner
Jeff Chandler
James Coburn
Joseph Cotten
Clark Gable
Stewart Granger
Van Heflin
Charlton Heston
William Holden
Rock Hudson
Walter Huston
Alan Ladd
Burt Lancaster
Dean Martin
Steve McQueen
Ray Milland
Robert Mitchum
Paul Newman
Jack Palance
Gregory Peck
Anthony Quinn
Robert Redford
Burt Reynolds
Robert Ryan
Robert Taylor
Barbara Stanwyck
Spencer Tracy
Richard Widmark
Joan Crawfiord
Audie Murphy
James Garner
William S. Hart
Harry Carey
Hoot Gibson
Richard Dix
George O'Brien
Lash LaRue
Errol Flynn
Jean Arthur
Kirk Douglas
Maureen O'Hara
Jane Russell

SUPPORTING PLAYERS
Lee Marvin
Claude Akins
Roy Roberts
Michael Pate
Anthony Quinn
James Best
L. Q. Jones
Strother Martin
Harry Carey, Jr.
Harry Dean Stanton
Bob Steele
Henry Brandon
R. G. Armstrong
John Anderson
Jack Elam
Gabby Hayes
Forrest Tucker
Rod Cameron
Henry Hull
Henry Morgan
Walter Brennan
Bruce Dern
Michael J. Pollard
Ken Curtis
Bo Hopkins
Ernest Borgnine
Edmond O'brien
Dub Taylor
Ben Johnson
Edger Buchanan
Chill Wills
Slim Pickens
Arthur Hunnicutt
J. Carrol Naish
Victor Jory
Jim Davis
Lee Van Cleef

APPENDIX T4:
Legendary Outlaws, Gunfighters And Lawmen

HENRY FONDA

"They say I killed six or seven men for snoring. Well, it ain't true, I only killed one man for snoring." — John Wesley Hardin

Who where the most desperate and notorious gunfighters of the Old West; men who had short and violent careers; who lead a brutal existence ending in violent death? Many ended up on the cover of a *Dime Novel* and became instant legends; their deeds exaggerated beyond reality, they were transported into the folklore of the American West? Below are some of those historical figures that have been portrayed in westerns over and over and over again.

TOP TEN MOST NOTORIOUS
Bill Longley
Ben Thompson
Billy the Kidd (William Bonney)
John Wesley Hardin
Jesse James
Clay Allison
Wild Bill Hickok (James Butler Hickok)
Black Jack Ketchum (Thomas Ketchum)
John Selman
Doc Holliday (John Henry Holliday)

BAD WOMEN
Poker Alice (Alice Tubbs)
Belle Starr (Myra Belle Shirley)
Cattle Kate (Ella Watson)
Calamity Jane (Martha Jane Canary)
Annie Oakley (Phoebe Anne Mozee)

NOTORIOUS INDIANS
Ned Christie
Sitting Bull (Tatanka Lyotake)
Crazy Horse
Geronimo (Goyathlay)
Cochise

NOTORIOUS LAWMEN
Pat Garrett
Dallas Stoudenmire
Heck Thomas
Charles A. Siringo
John Slaughter
Henry Starr
Wyatt Earp

MORE BADMEN
Frank James
Ben Thompson
Bitter Creek Newcomb
Sam Bass
The Youngers (John & Cole)
Luke Short
Black Bart (Charles E. Bolton)
Tom Horn
Jack Slade
William Clarke Quantrill
Bat Masterson (Bartholomew Masterson)
Ike Clanton
The Daltons (Robert, Emmett & Grattan)
Kit Carson
Jedediah Smith
Butch Cassidy (Robert Leroy Parker)
The Sundance Kid (Harry Longabaugh)
Kid Curry (Harvey Logan)

APPENDIX W1:
The Code Of The West

"The Code of the West: write it in your heart. Stand by the code, and it will stand by you. Ask no more and give no less than honesty, courage, loyalty, generosity, and fairness."
— Texas Bixbender, "Don't squat with yer spurs on"

One of the purposes of **RedRock Canyon Territory** is to preserve the value systems held by the men and women who settled the West. Values that helped make America a great country. Values that seem to be on the way out: Individual responsibility, honesty, integrity, honor, respect, self-reliance, "a days work for a days pay", and so forth. We have all heard the phrase "they lived by the Code of the West" but nowhere was that code written down. If it HAD been written down it might have looked something like the list below. It gives us a humorous but insightful look at those early American values.

THE CODE OF THE WEST
UNWRITTEN LAW OF THE WESTERN FRONTIER

1. **One should not** ask a stranger his name or where he comes from. His business is his own and you should not be too inquisitive about his past. He could be on the dodge.
2. **One should be hospitable** to a stranger come to town, for tomorrow he could be your neighbor.
3. **Always give your enemy** a fighting chance. Never shoot him in the back. A bushwacker is the lowest of cowards.
4. **A man's word must be good**, for there is no other contract. And calling another man a liar will surely have you leaning against a bullet!
5. **Under no circumstances** should you shoot an unarmed man, even if he is your bitter enemy. To do so is fair call for a hanging.
6. **One should not make threats** or insult a man without expecting dire consequences. And to be insulted is just cause for defending your honor.
7. **It is an insult** to offer to pay a host for your room and board. To make such an offer is to imply that he can't afford to have you as his guest.
8. **To steal a man's horse** is to ask for a stiff rope with a short drop. A man left stranded in an untamed wilderness without a means of conveyance is a man left for dead.
9. **It is to your good name** to honor and revere all women, be they farmers's wives or saloon girls, and never think of harming one hair of a woman.
10. **One should always look out for himself**, for it is no one elses duty but his own.

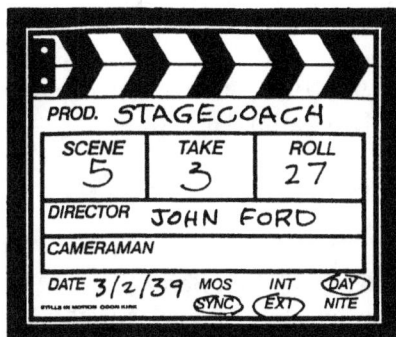

APPENDIX W2:
Television Westerns

"A fiery horse with the speed of light, a cloud of dust, and a hearty Hi-Yo Silver."
— opening line to TV's *Lone Ranger*, 1949-1965

Westerns were once regular TV fare. Do you remember these westerns and their stars? Some of the longest running series are listed below.

Bat Masterson, 1958-1961, Gene Barry (Bat Masterson).

The Big Valley, 1965-1969, Barbara Stanwyck (Victoria Barkley), Richard Long (Jarrod), Peter Breck (Nick), Lee Majors (Heath).

Bonanza, 1959-1973, Lorne Greene (Ben Cartwright), Michael Landon (Little Joe), Dan Blocker (Hoss), Pernell Roberts (Adam). TV's second longest running western.

Cheyenne, 1955-1963, Clint Walker (Cheyenne Bodie).

Death Valley Days, 1952-1970, hosted by Stanley Andrews, Ronald Reagan, Robert Taylor and Dale Robertson.

Gunsmoke, 1955-1975, James Arness (Matt Dillon), Amanda Blake (Kitty Russell), Dennis Weaver (Chester B. Goode), Milburn Stone (Doc Adams), Ken Curtis (Festus Haggen).

Have Gun, Will Travel, 1957-1963, Richard Boone (Paladin).

The High Chaparral, 1967-1971, Leif Erickson (John Cannon), Linda Cristal (Victoria Cannon), Cameron Mitchel (Buck Cannon), Mark Slade (Blue Cannon).

Hopalong Cassidy, 1949-1954, William Boyd (Hopalong Cassidy).

Kung Fu, 1972-1975, David Carradine (Kwai Chang Caine), Keye Luke (Master Po), Philip Ahn (Master Kan), Radames Pera (Grasshopper, the young Caine).

The Lawman, 1958-1962, John Russell (Marshal Dan Troop).

Little House On The Prairie, 1974-1983, Michael Landon (Charles Ingalls), Karen Grassle (Caroline Ingalls), Melissa Sue Anderson (Mary), Melissa Gilbert (Laura), Richard Bull (Nels Olseon), Katherine MacGregor (Harriet Oleson).

The Lone Ranger, 1949-1957, Clayton Moore (Lone Ranger), Jay Silverheels (Tonto).

Maverick, 1957-1962, James Garner (Bret Maverick), Jack Kelly (Bart Maverick).

Rawhide, 1959-1966, Eric Fleming (Gil Favor), Clint Eastwood (Rowdy Yates), Jim Murdock (Mushy), Paul Brinegar (Wishbone), Steve Raines (Quince).

The Rifleman, 1958-1963, Chuck Connors (Lucas McCain), Johnny Crawford (Mark).

Rin Tin Tin, 1954-1959, Lee Aaker (Rusty), Jim L. Brown (Lt. Ripley "Rip" Masters).

The Roy Rogers Show, 1951-1957, Roy Rogers, Dale Evans, Pat Brady, Sons of the Pioneers.

Sugarfoot, 1957-1960, Will Hutchins (Tom "Sugarfoot" Brewster).

Wagon Train, 1957-1965, Ward Bond (Major Seth Adams), John McIntire (Chris Hale), Robert Horton (Flint McCullough), Frank McGrath (Charlie Wooster), Terry Wilson (Bill Hawks).

Wanted - Dead or Alive, 1958-1961, Steve McQueen (Josh Randall).

Wells Fargo, 1957-1962, Dale Robertson (Jim Hardie), Jack Ging (Beau McCloud), Virginia Christine (Ovie), Lory Patrick (Tina), Mary Jane Saunders (Mary Gee), William Demarest (Jeb).

Wild Bill Hickok, 1951-1958, Guy Madison (U.S. Marshal James Butler), Andy Devine (Jingles B. Jones).

The Wild, Wild West, 1965-1969, Robert Conrad (James West), Ross Martin (Artemus Gordon).

The Virginian, 1962-1970, James Drury (The Virginian), Doug McClure (Trampas), Lee J. Cobb (Judge Henry Garth), Roberta Shore (Betsy Garth), L.Q. Jones (Belden), Harlan Warde (Sheriff Brannon).

Wyatt Earp, 1955-1961, Hugh O'Brian (Wyatt Earp), Douglas Fowley (Myron Healey), Morgan Woodward (Shotgun Gibbs).

The Young Riders, 1989-, Anthony Zerbe (Teaspoon Hunter), Ty Miller (The Kid), Stephen Baldwin (Billy Cody), Josh Brolin (Jimmy Hickok), Travis Fine (Ike McSwain), Gregg Rainwater (Buck Cross), Yvonne Suhor (Lou McCloud).

A few others with shorter runs:

Branded, 1965-1966, Chuck Connors (Jason McCord)

Cisco Kid, 1951-1953, Duncan Renaldo (Cisco Kid), Leo Carilo (Pancho).

Davy Crocket, 1954-1955, Fess Parker (Davy Crocket).

F Troop, 1965-1967, Ken Berry (Capt. Wilton Parmenter), Forrest Tucker (Sgt. Morgan O'Rourke), Larry Storch (Corporal Randolph Agarn), Melody Patterson (Wrangler Jane), Edward Everett Horton (Roaring Chicken), Frank Dekova (Wild Eagle).

The Guns Of Will Sonnett, 1967-1969, Walter Brennen (Will Sonnett), Dack Rambo (Jeff Sonnett), Jason Evers (Jim Sonnett).

Hondo, 1967, Ralph Taeger (Hondo Lane), Noah Beery,Jr.(Buffalo Baker), Gary Clarke (Captain Richards).

How The West Was Won, 1978-1979, James Arness (Zeb Macahan), Bruce Boxleitner (Luke), Kathryn Holcomb (Laura), Fionnula Flanagan (Molly Culhane), William Kirby Cullen (Jed Macahan), Vicki Schreck (Jessie).

Iron Horse, 1966-1968, Dale Robertson (Ben Calhoun), Gary Collins (Dave Tarrant), Bob Random (Barnabas Rogers), Roger Torrey (Nils Torvald), Ellen McRae (Julie Parsons).

The Lawman, 1958-1962, John Russell (Marshal Dam Troop), Peter Brown (Johnny Mckay), Bek Nelson (Dru Lemp), Barbara Long (Julie Tate), Peggie Castle (Lily Merrill).

Paradise, 1988-1991, Lee Horsley (Ethan Allen Cord), Jenny Beck (Claire Carroll).

Lawman, 1958-1962, John Russell (Marshal Dan Troop), Peter Brown (Johnny Mckay), Bek Nelson (Dru Lemp), Barbara Long (Julie Tate), Peggie Castle (Lily Merrill).

APPENDIX W3:
Top Western Movies

"The western is a haunting form. It's useful dramatically because it's so simple: good and evil, men and nature, earth and sky. But there's more to it than that. Westerns have a lot to do with the myth that is still America, and so long as that myth survives, so will the western."
— James Monaco

Some of the best western movies ever made are listed below. They are in alphabetical order and are listed by title first, then director, date, and lead actor. Critics and western fans will have different opinions as to how many "stars" these westerns should be honored with, but most will agree that those listed below stand out among the thousands of "A" and "B" westerns that were produced. The list includes not only the classics but also the better "B" westerns.

FIVE STAR WESTERNS

Dances With Wolves, Kevin Costner, 1990, Kevin Costner.
The Grey Fox, Philip Borsos, 1982, Richard Farnsworth.
The Gunfighter, Henry King, 1950, Gregory Peck.
High Noon, Fred Zinnemann, 1952, Gary Cooper.
The Man Who Shot Liberty Valance, John Ford, 1962, John Wayne.
Once Upon A Time In The West, Sergio Leone, 1969, Claudia Cardinale.
The Searchers, John Ford, 1950, John Wayne.
Shane, George Stevens, 1953, Alan Ladd.
She Wore A Yellow Ribbon, John Ford, 1949, John Wayne.
Stagecoach, John Ford, 1939, John Wayne.
The Tall T, Budd Boetticher, 1957, Randolph Scott.

FOUR STAR WESTERNS

The Ballad Of Cable Hogue, Sam Peckinpah, 1970, Jason Robards, Jr.
Bite The Bullit, Richard Brooks, 1975, Gene Hackman.
Butch Cassidy And The Sundance Kid, George Roy Hill, 1969, Paul Newman.
The Cheyenne Social Club, Gene Kelly, 1970, James Stewart.
The Cowboys, Mark Rydell, 1972, John Wayne.
El Dorado, Howard Hawks, 1967, John Wayne.
Fort Apache, John Ford, 1948, John Wayne.
The Last Outlaw, Christy Cabanne, 1936, Harry Carey.
The Man From Laramie, Anthony Mann, 1955, James Stewart.
McCabe And Mrs. Miller, Robert Altman, 1971, Warren Beatty.
My Darling Clementine, John Ford, 1946, Henry Fonda.

The Naked Spur, Anthony Mann, 1953, James Stewart.
The Outlaw Josey Wales, Clint Eastwood, 1976, Clint Eastwood.
Pat Garrett And Billy The Kid, Sam Peckinpah, 1973, James Coburn.
Ride Lonesome, Bud Boetticher, 1959, Randolph Scott.
Ride The High Country, Sam Peckinpah, 1962, Joel McCrea.
Rio Bravo, Howard Hawks, 1959, John Wayne.
The Shootist, Don Siegel, 1976, John Wayne.
Silverado, Lawrence Kasdan, 1985, Kevin Kline.
Support Your Local Sheriff, Burt Kennedy, 1969, James Garner.
Unforgiven, Clint Eastwood, 1992, Clint Eastwood.
Wagonmaster, John Ford, 1950, Ben Johnson.
The Wild Bunch, Sam Peckinpah, 1969, William Holden.
Will Penny, Tom Gries, 1968, Charlton Heston.

THREE STAR WESTERNS

Along Came Jones, Stuart Heisler, 1945, Gary Cooper.
Angel And The Badman, James Edward Grant, 1947, John Wayne.
Bend Of The River, Anthony Mann, 1952, James Stewart.
Arizona Legion, David Howard, 1939, George O'Brien.
Bad Company, Robert Benton, 1972, Jeff Bridges.
The Ballad Of Gregorio Cortez, Robert M. Young, 1982, Edward James Olmos.
Barbarosa, Fred Schepisi, 1982, Willie Nelson.
Brimstone, Joseph Kane, 1949, Rod Cameron.
Broken Lance, Edward Dmytryk, 1954, Spencer Tracy.
Caravan Trail, Robert Emmett Tansey, 1946, Eddie Dean.
Cariboo Trail, Edwin L. Marin, 1950, Randolph Scott.
Carson City Cyclone, Howard Bretherton, 1943, Don Berry.
The Comancheros, Michael Curtiz, 1961, John Wayne.
Come On Tarzan, Alan James, 1932, Ken Maynard.
Comes A Horseman, Alan J. Pakula, 1978, Jane Fonda.
Coroner Creek, Ray Enright, 1948, Randolph Scott.
Daniel Boone, David Howard, 1936, George O'Brien.
Dark Command, Raoul Walsh, 1940, John Wayne.
Days Of Old Cheyenne, Elmer Clifton, 1943, Don Barry.
Destry Rides Again, George Marshal, 1939, James Stewart.
Dodge City, Michael Curtiz, 1939, Errol Flynn.
Doolins Of Oklahoma, Gordon Douglas, 1949, Randolph Scott.
End Of The Trail, D. Ross Lederman, 1932, Tim McCoy.
Enemy Of The Law, Harry Fraser, 1945, Tex Ritter.
Flaming Star, Don Siegel, 1960, Elvis Presley.
The Good, The Bad And The Ugly, Sergio Leone, 1966, Clint Eastwood.
Gunfight At The O.K. Corral, John Sturges, 1957, Burt Lancaster.
Heart Of The Rockies, Joseph Kane, 1937, Robert Livingston.
Heartland, Richard Pearce, 1979, Con Chata Ferrell.
Hombre, Martin Ritt, 1967, Paul Newman.
Hondo, John Farrow, 1953, John Wayne.
The Horse Soldiers, John Ford, 1959, John Wayne.
Jeremiah Johnson, Sydney Pollack, 1972, Robert Redford.
The Last Of The Mohicans, George B. Seitz, 1936, Randolph Scott.
Law And Order, Edward L. Cahn, 1932, Walter Huston.
Lawless Valley, Bert Gilroy, 1938, George O'Brien.
Lightnin' Crandall, Sam Newfield, 1937, Bob Steele.

Little Big Horn, Charles Marquis Warren, 1951, Lloyd Bridges.
Little Big Man, Arthur Penn, 1970, Dustin Hoffman.
Loney Are The Brave, David Miller, 1962, Kirk Douglas.
The Lusty Men, Nicholas Ray, 1952, Robert Mitchum.
The Magnificent Seven, John Sturges, 1960, Yul Brynner.
The Man From Snowy River, George Miller, 1982, Tom Burlinson.
Man In The Saddle, Andre de Toth, 1951, Randolph Scott.
Man Of The Forest, Henry Hathaway, 1933, Randolph Scott.
Man Of The West, Anthony Mann, 1958, Gary Cooper.
Marshal Of Cripple Creek, R.G. Springsteen, 1947, Allan "Rocky" Lane.
Marshall Of Mesa City, David Howard, 1939, George O'Brien.
Mexicali Rose, George Sherman, 1939, Gene Autry.
The Missourians, George Blair, 1950, Monte Hale.
North To Alaska, Henry Hathaway, 1960, John Wayne.
One-Eyed Jacks, Marlon Brando, 1961, Marlon Brando.
The Ox-Bow Incident, William Wellman, 1943, Henry Fonda.
Pony Express Rider, Hal Harrison, 1976, Stewart Peterson.
Quigley Down Under, Simon Wincer, 1990, Tom Selleck.
Rage At Dawn, Tim Whelan, 1955, Randolph Scott.
Range Feud, D. Ross Lederman, 1931, Buck Jones.
Red River, Howard Hawks, 1948, John Wayne.
Renegade Ranger, David Howard, 1938, George O'Brien.
Riders Of The Rio Grande, Howard Bretherton, 1943, Bob Steele.
Rio Grande, John Ford, 1950, John Wayne.
The Rustlers, Lesley Selander, 1949, Tim Holt.
Santa Fe Saddlemates, Thomas Carr, 1945, Sunset Carson.
Santa Fe Uprising, R.G. Springsteen, 1946, Allan "Rocky" Lane.
Shenandoah, Andrew V. McLaglen, 1965, James Stewart.
Short Grass, Lesley Selander, 1950, Rod Cameron.
Skin Game, Paul Bogart, 1971, James Garner.
South Of St. Louis, Ray Enright, 1949, Merlene Dietrich.
The Spoilers, Ray Enright, 1942, Marlene Dietrich.
Stampede, Lesley Selander, 1949, Rod Cameron.
Stone Of Silver Creek, Nick Grinde, 1935, Buck Jones.
The Sundown Rider, Lambert Hillyer, 1933, Buck Jones.
Tall In The Saddle, Edwin L. Marlin, 1944, John Wayne.
Texas Cyclone, D. Ross Lederman, 1932, Tim McCoy.
Texas Masquerade, George Archain Baud, 1944, William Boyd.
The Texas Rangers, Phil Karlson, 1951, George Nelson.
Thousand Pieces of Gold, Nancy Kelly, 1991, Rosalind Chao.
3:10 To Yuma, Delmer Daves, 1957, Glenn Ford.
The Tin Star, Anthony Mann, 1957, Henry Fonda.
To The Last Man, Henry Hathaway, 1933, Randolph Scott.
Trail Drive, Alan James, 1933, Ken Maynard.
True Grit, Henry Hathaway, 1969, John Wayne.
Two-Fisted Law, D. Ross Lederman, 1932, Tim McCoy.
Ulzana's Raid, Robert Aldrich, 1972, Burt Lancaster.
The Virginian, Victor Fleming, 1929, Gary Cooper.
The Westerner, William Wyler, 1940, Gary Cooper.
When A Man Sees Red, Alan James, 1934, Buck Jones.
Wild Frontier, Phillip Ford, 1947, Allan "Rocky" Lane.
The Wild Rovers, Blake Edwards, 1971, William Holden.
Wild West, Robert Emmett Tansey, 1946, Eddie Dean.
Windwalker, Keith Merrill, 1980, Trevor Howard.

APPENDIX W4:
Western Movie Trivia

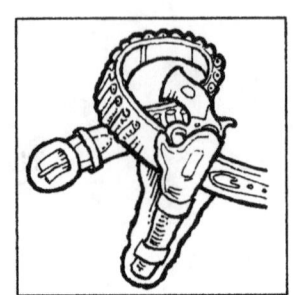

"A man's gotta do what a man's gotta do."
— Aland Ladd, *Shane*, 1953.

Here are a few classic trivia questions to wet the appetitie of western film buffs.

John Wayne won only one Oscar in his career. For what film was it? TRUE GRIT, 1969 for Best Actor playing "Rooster Cogburn". He was nominated for an Oscar for *Sands of Iwo Jima* but didn't win.

How many sequels were there to the enormously successful western "The Magnificent Seven", directed in 1960 by John Sturges and starring Yul Brynner? THREE: *Return Of The Seven*, 1966, *Guns Of The Magnificent Seven*, 1969, and *The Magnificent Seven Ride!*, 1972.

Who said the most memorable line in Western fiction: "When you call me that, smile!"? It was first said by "THE VIRGINIAN" in Owen Wister's 1902 novel *The Virginian* after he was challenged at a poker game by the loosing villain *Trampas* who snarled: "Your bet, you son-of-a-bitch". Gary Cooper also said a similar line in the 1929 movie version of the novel; "If you want to call me that, smile."

Who was the "Man With No Name"? CLINT EASTWOOD in Sergio Leone's "Spagheti Westerns": *Fistful Of Dollars*, 1964, *For A Few Dollars More*, 1965, and *The Good, The Bad and The Ugly*, 1966. He was described as unshaven, a serape draped over his shoulders, a flat-crowned hat shading his narrowed eyes and a half-smoked cigarillo drooping from the corner of his mouth."

Lee Marvin played two parts in the 1965 hit "Cat Ballou" and won the oscar for Best Actor that year. What were the names of the two characters he played? He played twin brothers: an amiable drunk named "KID SHELEEN" and a sadistic killer with a silver nose who called himself "TIM STRAWN."

What was John Wayne's real name? The Duke was originally given the name MARION ROBERT MORRISON but when his younger brother "Robert" was born his middle name was changed to MICHAEL. Wayne got the name "Duke" when, as a kid, he went everywhere with his large airedale terrior named "Duke", so everyone called the dog "Big Duke" and Marion "Little Duke"!

What was Charles Bronson's real name? Bronson was born "CHARLES BUCHINSKY."

Who played Marshal Dillon's (James Arnez) deputy on the long running television series "Gunsmoke"? There were two: Starting in 1955 DENNIS WEAVER played the gimpy-legged "Chester Good" and in 1964 KEN CURTIS took over the part as "Festus Hagen."

Return to the thrilling days of yesteryear: who played the Lone Ranger's (Clayton Moore) faithful Indian Companion "Tonto" in the "Lone Ranger" television series in the 1950's? Tonto was played by JAY SILVERHEELS. He was also in several movies: Two Lone Ranger movies in 1956 and 1958: *Broken Arrow* in 1950 and *Santee* in 1973.

What western TV series did William Shatner (of Star Trek fame) star in, in the mid 1970's? "THE BARBARY COAST". Only thirteen episodes were aired in 1975. Shatner played "Jeff Cable, Special Agent".

Henry Fonda only played one role as a villain. What western was it in? Fonda played a hired killer in the classic spagetti western "ONCE UPON A TIME IN THE WEST", directed by Sergio Leone in 1969. It also starred Claudia Cardinale, Charles Bronson and Jason Robarts.

Did John Wayne ever die in any of his movies? If so which one(s)? YES, John Wayne died in THREE of his movies: *The Shootist* in 1976, his last movie where he plays a famous gunfighter dying of cancer, *The Cowboys* in 1972 where he plays a rancher on a cattle drive dogged by a vengeful outlaw, and *The Alamo* where he plays Davy Crocket at the battle of the Alamo, and we all know what happened there.

What were the names of Ben Cartright's (Lorne Greene) three sons in the long running TV western "Bonanza"? HOSS (Dan Blocker), LITTLE JOE (Michael Landon), and ADAM (Pernell Roberts).

From what classic western movie did this quote come from: "Kid, the next time I say, 'Lets go someplace like Bolivia, lets GO some place like Bolivia!'"? BUTCH CASSIDY AND THE SUNDANCE KID (1969). It was said by Paul Newman to Robert Redford just before jumping off a cliff into a raging river. They had been "dogged" by a relentless posse for days and had finally reached a canyon ledge with nowhere to go but down.

What western detective had this slogan on his business card: "Have Gun, Will Travel"? PALADIN, played by Richard Boone in the TV western "Have Gun, Will Travel" in 1957 through 1963. His business card bore the image of a chess knight and read: "Have Gun, Will Travel. Wire Paladin, San Francisco."

APPENDIX W5:
Quotes From Westerns

Below is listed a few lines of dialogue from some of your favorite westerns. Can you correctly guess the TITLE of the movie from which the quote was taken? Answers at the bottom of page.

1. "When you get to disliking someone, he ain't around for long."
2. "Who are those guys?"
3. "Badges! We ain't got no badges. We don't need no badges. I don't have to show you any stinking badges."
4. "Joey, don't get to liking Shane too much. He'll be moving on one day."
5. "I've been given command of the armies of Texas, but the fly in the buttermilk is there ain't no armies in Texas."
6. "Always uses top grade hemp, Schmidt does. Oils it so it slides real good. Snap your neck like a dried-out twig."
7. "You just keep thinking, Butch. That's what you're good at."
8. "A band of hostile Comanche came through a week ago. I asked if there was a white girl with 'em - they got sullen and suspicious."
9. "Keep Santa Anna off the back of my neck until I can get in shape to fight him."
10. "That one in the center, he was in no itching hurry. But that one on the far left, he had crazy eyes. I figured him to make the first move."
11. "Think you used enough dynamite, Butch?"
12. "Somebody back East is saying, 'Why don't he write?'"
13. "You a bounty hunter? Dying ain't much of a living, boy."
14. "How can you trust a man who wears both a belt AND suspenders? The man doesn't even trust his own pants!"
15. "You don't remember me do ya . . . when you hang a man you better look at him."

ANSWERS: **1:** *The Outlaw Josey Wales*, **2:** *Butch Cassidy And The Sundance Kid*, **3:** *Treasure Of The Sierra Madre*, **4:** *Shane*, **5:** *The Alamo*, **6:** *Hang 'Em High*, **7:** *Butch Cassidy And The Sundance Kid*, **8:** *The Searchers*, **9:** *The Alamo*, **10:** *The Outlaw Josey Wales*, **11:** *Butch Cassidy And The Sundance Kid*, **12:** *Dances With Wolves*, **13:** *The Outlaw Josey Wales*, **14:** *Once Upon A Time In The West*, **15:** *Hang 'Em High*.

APPENDIX W6:
Why The Old West?

"The images, language, and myths of the frontier experience pervade nearly every aspect of American life . . . Although other nations regard frontiers as boundaries, to Americans the word calls up *wide open spaces* and a *promise of unlimited oppoprtunity*."
— Martin Ridge, *Atlas of the American Frontiers*, 1993

What makes the Old West attractive to millions? Why does the Western movie, over all other types of films, have such a hold on our imagination? In 1845, Daniel Webster had this to say about the western wilderness: "What do we want with this region of savages and wild beasts, of deserts, of shifting sands and whirlwinds of dust, of cactus and prairie dogs? . . .To what use could we ever put those endless mountain ranges? What could we do with the western coast line three thousand miles away, rockbound, cheerless and uninviting?" Surprise, surprise, the desire to better oneself and provide something better for one's children is a strong driving force. That force created a frontier settlement that was unique to the world and has fascinated people around the world ever since. But why? Listed below are a couple of quotes from various historians of the American West that may give the reader some idea. ***RedRock Canyon Territory*** will be successful because it will fill some of the needs of the American people:

> There will always be an audience for the western, for the western represents romantic adventure and idealism, achievement, optimism for the future, justice, individualism, the beauty of the land, and the courage and independence of the individuals who won the land. It is the western that the American discovers himself again as one of the decendants of a people who knew how to work hard, who knew how to fight, who where prepared to die. This is all in contrast to the padded world in which the American so often finds himself today; the land is a little bit further away, and the day of the horse has passed.
> — **George Fenin**, *The Western*, 1962

> Out of the Frontier West the American character was formed - a people audacious and self-reliant and naive, generous and stubborn, righteous but forgiving, homorous in a folksy way, violent, hospitable, contradictory.
> — **Dee Brown**, *The Wild West*, 1993

With the settling of most wilderness areas, the concept of the frontier has come to symbolize a STATE OF MIND where the *human imagination is free to explore and create,* unhindered by what has been done in the past. Confronted with the problems of their society and the challenge of living within the limited resources of the earth, Americans are reinterpreting this frontier legacy. Yet its spirit can continue to inspire succeeding ingenuity and courage.
— **Martin Ridge**, *Atlas of the American Frontiers*, 1993

Everybody is aware that the western is responding to a basic need, but nobody tells us exactly what it is. I suggest that this basic need is a natural and normal hunger for a heroic past. We want to have roots in ancient times like other peoples, but we don't stay in one place long enough to grow them . . . Many of us know nothing about our own grandfathers. Pride of family is denied to all but a few of us. Pride of race has to be built. Any group with a thousand-year history has these things provided, but the American is a newcomer and not yet completely at home in his vast country, all he has is the mystical West, and he needs it desperately.
— **C.L. Sonnichsen**, "The West That Wasn't", *American West* magazine, Nov / Dec 1977.

We are fascinated by the outlaw, with or without a badge, because "more that any other he embodies the secret loneliness in all our hearts, the uninhibited lust for violence, the naked fear, the relentless unrest".
— **Frank Waters**, *American West* magazine, Nov / Dec, 1977.

When the ganster is killed, his whole life is shown to have been a mistake, but the image the westerner seeks to maintain can be presented as clearly in defeat as in victory: He fights not for advantage and not for the right, but to state what he is, and he must live in a world which permits that statement. The westerner is the last gentleman, and the movies which over and over again tell his story are probably the last art form in which the concept of honor retains its strength.
— **Robert Warshow**, *Movie Chronicle: The Westerner*

The West was wild for a time, ruthless and tragic, but it was glorious, too, the greatest and swiftest movement of mass settlement across a continent in the world's history, resulting in clashes between good and evil forces that reverberate to this day.
— **Dee Brown**, *The Wild West*, 1993

To the frontier the American intellect owes its striking characteristics. That coarseness and strength combined with acuteness and inquisitiveness; that practical, inventive turn of mind, quick to find expedients; that masterful grasp of material things, lacking in the artistic but powerful to effect great ends; that restless nervous energy; that dominant individualism working for good or evil and withal that buoyancy and exuberance which comes with freedom - these are the traits of the frontier.
— **Frederick Jackson Turner**, *The Significance of the Frontier in American History*, 1893

It is not violence at all which is the 'point' of the Western movie, but a certain image of man, a style, which expresses itself most clearly in violence, watch a child with his toy guns and you will see: what most interests him is not (as we so much fear) the fantasy of hunting others, but to work out how a man might look when he shoots or is shot. A hero is one who looks like a hero.
— **Robert Warshow**, *Movie Chronicle: The Westerner*

The road to the stars has been discovered none too soon. Civilization cannot exist without new frontiers; it needs them both physically and spiritually. The physical need is obvious - new lands, new resources, new materials. The spiritual need is less apparent, but in the long run it is more important. We do not live by bread alone; we need adventure, variety, novelty, romance. As the psychologists have shown by their sensory deprivation experiments, a man goes swiftly mad if he is isolated in a silent, darkened room, cut off completely from the external world. What is true of individuals is also true of societies; they too can become insane without sufficient stimulus.
— **Arthur C. Clarke**, *Profiles Of The Future*, Sept. 1977.

... and it was as if nothing affected people in those days. They threw themselves blindly into the impossible, and accomplished the unbelievable. If anyone succumbed in the struggle—and that happened often—another would come and take his place. Youth was in the race; the unknown, the untried, the unheard-of, was in the air; people caught it, were intoxicated by it, threw themselves away, and laughed at the cost. Of course it was possible out here.
— **O.E. Rolvagg**, *Giants in the Earth*, 1927

No figure has dominated American romantic folklore like the legendary cowboy. Daring, noble, ethical, romantic, he permeates our popular media to this very day. He personifies our national self-image—the conqueror of wilderness, savagery, and villainy. He is America's knight-errant with a colt .45 . . . The national hero-worship of the westerner is based on needs within American society which cause us to reproduce the cowboy legend generation after generation through our popular mass media."
— **Richard A. Maynard**, *The American West on Film: Myth & Reality*, 1974

The effectiveness of the western as a genre has scarcely depended upon fidelity of detail or, for that matter, upon emotional validity. Hollywood surely would have been foolish to attempt to do the American cowboy or the winning of the West realistically; applying an anti-romantic technique to an essentially romantic subject would have amounted to a sort of alchemical reverse english; it would have been deliberately turning gold into lead. The cowboy (or the gunfghter), whatever he may be in real life, lives in the American imagination as a mythic figure, or at least a figure of high romance; his legend, however remotely it may relate to his day-to-day existence, is still one of the most widely compelling of our diminishing number of national legends.
— **Larry McMurtry**, *The American West On Film*

APPENDIX G1:
Glossary Of Architectural Terms

The choice of architectural styles in the West was made by men who wanted to bring a more citified eastern look to their raw frontier towns. They copied details from the new Victorian-era architecture popular in the East. But they found these designs had to be adapted to the needs of the West and a new architecture was born: the false-fronted buildings that have now become a symbol of the American West.

BALLOON FRAMING: A method of construction where small dimensional lumber runs vertically from sill to eaves and horizontal siding can be nailed to it allowing great flexibility in design. A development that greatly promoted the growth of towns in the West.

BALUSTRADE: A row of turned or rectangular posts joined by a rail, serving as an enclosure for balconies, staircases, terraces, etc.

BOARD-AND-BATTEN: Vertical plank siding with joints covered by narrow wood strips.

BRACKET: A traingular-shapped decorative element used under a cornice and appears to support it.

CHINKING: Mud, grass, etc. used to fill the spaces between the logs of a cabin.

CLAPBOARD: Board siding laid horizontally and overlapping, butted vertically.

CORNICE: A decoratively treated horizontal moulding at the edge of a roof.

DORMER: A window placed vertically in a sloping roof and which has a roof of its own.

FACADE: The exterior face of a building.

FENESTRATION: The arrangement of windows in a building.

GABLE: The triangular upper portion of a wall at the end of a pitched roof.

GINGERBREAD: Fancy wood carvings on furniture, front porches, etc. applied to Victorian houses.

LINTEL: A horizontal beam of wood, stone or steel that bridges the top of a window or door opening to support the load above it.

MANSARD ROOF: A roof with two slopes on each of the four sides, the lower steeper than the upper.

PLACITA: In New Mexico, a courtyard encircled by the wings of a house or by several houses.

QUOINING: Heavy blocks, generally of stone, or of wood cut to imitate stone, used at each corner of a building to reinforce masonry walls, or in wood or brick as a decorative feature.

WAINSCOT: Wood paneling applied to the lower part of an interior wall.

VIGA: A log with the bark peeled off, used as a ceiling beam. Usually seen protruding through the outside walls of southwestern adobe buildings.

APPENDIX G2:
Glossary Of Motion Picture Terms

The language of the filmmaker is as unique as any trade's jargon. Ever wonder what those credits at the end of a movie mean? A "foley" or "focus puller"? Because moviemaking is an integral part of *RedRock Canyon*, a few "film" words, some used used in this proposal, are included here.

ART DIRECTOR: The person knowledgeable in design and architecture who supervises construction of the *sets*.

ASSISTANT DIRECTOR: The director's right-hand man who manages the set: keeps it orderly, supervises extras, makes sure all departments are ready when a shot is scheduled, and sees that "call" (time and location) is known by the crew for the next day's shooting.

ATMOSPHERE: The extras used in the background of a *scene* to add realism, like the people walking on a city street.

BEST BOY: Second in command to either the *Gaffer* or *Key Grip*; he is the "best of the crew" and is ready to take on his bosses job and lead the rest of the crew in their department.

BREAKAWAY: Set pieces like furniture, chairs, bottles, windows, etc. designed to fall apart easily when thrown, hit, or run into.

CAMERA ANGLE: The placement of the camera in relation to the subject being photographed. A wide angle might show the whole room, while a closeup will show only the face of an actor or focus on a single object. A "high angle" looks down on the subject while a "low angle" (camera near the floor) looks up on the subject.

CONTINUITY: The smooth flow of action from shot to shot and scene to scene. Scenes aren't shot in sequence when a movie is made, so a "script supervisor" has to keep track of dialog, the way actor's are dressed, the direction they look off screen, *props* and *set dressing* in the scene to make sure things don't "jump around" in a scene once *shots* are *cut* together.

CUT: The announcement by the director when he feels the scene is over and the camera and sound machine can be stopped. He'll usually say "print it" and move onto the next shot or "that was perfect, do another one for safety." The word is also used in other ways like "to cut the film"(edit the film), "to cut to another *camera angel* (to change to)."

DAILIES: The scenes photographed the day before, are processed and printed in a lab, and then projected in a small theatre, so the director, cinematographer, editor, etc. can see if scenes need to be re-shot before tearing down sets or changing locations.

DOLLY: A moveable, wheeled platform on which is mounted the camera and seats for the camera operator and assistant so the camera can be moved around the set while shooting a scene.

DRESSING THE SET: To furnish a room or location with furniture, draperies, artwork, glassware, flowers, etc. to complete the impression and make the set look as real as possible. Dressing is carefully chosen to be appropriate to the time period and character(s) inhabiting the place.

FOCUS PULLER: The "first assistant cameraman" who's primary job is to adjust the focus during a shot. He also maintains the camera and changes lenses.

FOLEY ARTIST: The person who's job it is during post production to create sounds for each scene that were not recorded during principal photography, He might have to create footfalls, creaking doors, clothing sounds, and the like while viewing a final cut of the film.

GAFFER: The chief electrician on the set who leads a crew who's job it is to provide all the electricity to lights and equipment on the set. They are in charge of all cabling, electrical generators, "tie-ins" to house power, etc.

GRIP: A crewmember who provides the labor on a set. Lighting grips setup and rig lights; a dolly grip sets up track and moves the *dolly* during a shot.

HOT SET: A set that has been dressed and is ready for shooting. Signs are sometimes put up so the crew will know that props, decorations, etc. are not to be touched, nor is grip and lighting equipment to be stored there.

LOCATION: Any setting used for filming that is away from the studio and is not a constructed set. The cast and crew will have to go "on location" to *shoot* the film. The production managers must bring food, shelter, and toilet facilities to the location, which might be on the other side of the world from the studio.

PROP: Short for property, Any moveable object used by an actor in a scene as opposed to things that are only there as background *dressing*.

QUIET ON THE SET: The call given by the assistant director before the camera is about to roll, to make sure no sound is heard when the action starts.

SCENE: A single shot or series of shots making up a piece of action or which occurs at a single location.

SET: Short for setting, it's and indoor or outdoor location that has been constructed to look like a real place. A room may have only two walls, a building may be just a wall propped up from behind, but with the addition of *dressing* and lighting looks real. Rooms usually have no ceiling to allow placement of lights, and walls can sometimes be moved to make room for camera and crew.

SHOOT: To photograph a scene in a motion picture or television show. Crew members also refer to a film project they are working on as "a shoot."

SHOT: The single uninterrupted operation of the camera that records one piece of action. The basic building block of a film. Shots are edited together to make scenes or sequences in a film. Also called a "take."

SLATE: The hinged wooden board that is photographed at the beginning of every take so that the film and sound can be "synched up" in the editing room. When the top piece of the slate is brought down, it makes a sound and can be matched with the picture of the boards coming together. The slate is also used to write information needed for identifying the take: *scene* and *shot* number, camera roll number, director and name of film. Also called clapperboard or clapsticks.

STEADICAM: A trade name for a gimbaled devise that allows holding a camera and walking with it so there is no camera shake. It allows the operator to travel over rough terrain, along narrow hallways and up stairways where a *dolly* or crane mounted camera could not go. Panavision, a camera manufacturing company, developed a similar device called the Panaglide.

STORYBOARD: A visual representation of the film to be shot that looks much like a cartoon strip, each frame representing a shot in the movie. It allows everyone involved in the production to get an idea of what will be required in sets, special effects, special camera setups, etc.

APPENDIX G3:
Glossary Of Mining Terms

The discovery of gold and silver in the American West made a significant contribution to it's rapid settlement. As in any profession, special terminology is needed to define the materials and operations of placer and hard rock mining.

ADIT: The horizontal opening giving access to the vertical shaft of a mine and by which water and ores can be carried away.

ASSAY: To determine the metal content of a mineral or ore.

BONANZA: A Spanish term signifying good luck or prosperity; a rich vein or pocket of ore or anything which yeilds a large income.

COLOR: Those tiny particles of gold that appear after shaking out a gold pan.

CRIBBING: Heavy-timbered cratelike construction used to support structures on sloping sites.

DREDGE: A mechanical or hydraulic device used to dig up creek and river beds to find gold. The gravel is fed into sluices to separate the color.

FLUME: Boxing or piping for conveying water.

GRUBSTAKE: To provide a miner with food and supplies in exchange for a portion of the findings of his prospecting.

HARDROCK MINING: Mining where drilling and blasting is required to break up the rock to get at the valuable ore.

HEADFRAME: A metal or timber frame, with a large pulley at the top and situated over a mine shaft that allows the cage containing men and materials to be hoisted up out of the ground.

HOIST SHACK: The building behind the *headframe* which houses the hoist winch and power source.

LODE: A fissure filled with ore-bearing matter. The Mother Lode is the biggest and original source of all the other rich deposits.

PAY DIRT: Dirt rich in precious minerals.

PANNING: To use a gold pan to separate gold from the sand or gravel at the bottom of creeks and rivers.

PLACER MINING: The mining of waterborne or glacial deposits of gravel or sand containing heavy ore minerals such as gold, platinum, etc. which have been eroded from their original bedrock and concentrated as small particles that can be washed out.

SHAFT: A vertical (or slanted) tunnel giving access to underground mining operations.

SLUICE BOX: A trough through which gold-bearing gravel is washed.

STAMP MILL: A mechanical device that uses large weights on a camshaft to crush ore in order to get at the valuable minerals.

TAILING: Waste or refuse in various processes of milling, mining, distilling, etc.

TIMBERING: The wooden supports and braces used to "shore up" or stabilize mine tunnels and underground workings.

APPENDIX G-4:
Glossary Of Railroad Terms

As in any profession, the railroad has its own colorful language to describe the people, things and activities it is involved in. Listed here is a sampling of terms and slang phrases to wet your appetite to the life of the railroader.

ANGEL'S SEAT: Also *crow's nest* or *penthouse*. The CUPOLA or observation tower of a caboose. From that vantage point it was possible for the brakeman to spot hot journals, brake beams that had dropped down, and other dangers.

BALLAST: The slag or gravel used to hold the crossties in place after the rails have been spiked to them.

BEANERY: A railroad eating establishment.

BEDBUG: Slang for the Pullman porter.

BOXCAR TOURIST: A hobo *riding the rods*.

BRAKEMAN: The crewman who's job it is to take care of the brakes and couplings, to signal and flag trains, and generally to oversee the cars under the direction of the conductor. In the early days of railroading, he had to climb on top of cars and jump on and off the moving train. He had to run ahead of an engine, throw a switch, and stand there until the train had passed. He had to work in the rain, snow, and sleet. If he was a rear brakeman, he had to go back some distance behind the train and flag a following train, no matter how bad the weather. And he was the lowest-paid crewman!

BRASS BUTTONS: A passenger train conductor.

BUG: The sending instrument of the telegrapher. Many operators carried their own personal "key" adjusted to their touch.

BUZZARD'S ROOST: Slang for the YARDMASTER'S OFFICE which was up on a tower so he could see the whole yard.

CINDER TRAIL: The hobo's term for the railroad right-of-way. CINDERS are partly burned pieces of coal capable of further burning without flame. Cinder dust is seen flying from the smoke stack and getting into passenger's eyes.

CONSIST: The conductor's report, sent by telegraph, to the next station telling the yardmaster the MAKEUP OF THE TRAIN: types of cars, destinations of the freight, etc. so he can plan switching operations.

COWCATCHER: The out-thrusted, wrought-iron bars on the front of the engine designed to push cattle off the track. Before it's invention, cattle would get caught under the engine and cause its derailment.

CRUMMY: Slang name for the CABOOSE. There were many other names for the car at the end of the train where the conductor took care of his paperwork, the train crew prepared their meals, the stockman rode when traveling with a shipment of cattle, and the brakeman rode to protect the rear of the train. Some other names: *angel's seat, ape wagon, crow's nest, penthouse,* and *skunk speeder.*

CUSHIONS: Slang for a passenger car.

DISPATCHER: The railroad employee who has the critical job of controlling the movement of the trains. He must keep track of where each train is, where trains are to meet to pass, and how much time one or the other has lost.

DOUBLEHEADER: A train hauled by two engines, usually needed in the mountains and during heavy snows.

FIREMAN: The crewman whose job it was to keep up steam by shoveling coal into the firebox, placing the coal evenly to prevent smoke. He sat on the left side of the cab, and it was his duty to watch that side of the track, ring the bell, keep the cab clean, wash the widows, and keep coal handy to the firebox. He had to stoke the fire and maintain the water level in the boiler. His was the job of hopeful apprenticeship to becoming an engineer.

GANDY DANCER: A right of way laborer, so called because many of the tools used by the section gangs were made by the *Gandy Manufacturing Company of Chicago.*

HANDCAR: A platform with four flanged wheels propelled by a two-handled pump. It was used in the early days to carry section crews along the right of way to make repairs. It was light enough to be lifted off the track to avoid a collision with a passing train. Later gas driven cars called *speeders* were used.

HIGHBALL: A signal given by the conductor or brakeman by waving a hand or lantern in a high, wide semicircle, meaning "leave town" or "full speed ahead".

HOMESTEAD: To jump off a runaway train.

JERKWATER: A small town, because taking on water was the only reason for stopping. In refilling the tender, the fireman would pull down on the tank's spout and "jerk water".

NEWS BUTCH: The peddler on early-day passenger trains who walked up and down the isles selling candy, newspapers, fruit, peanuts, racy magazines, coffee, cigars, and soap; all the necessities for surviving those long arduous trips. The *butch* was a business man: he would go through the train selling salted peanuts and then return with cold, bottled drinks. At the end of a run, he would gather up all the used newspapers and resell them to the newly boarded passengers!

OLD GIRL: A steam locomotive, a term of affection. A locomotive is referred to as "she" not "it."

PULLMAN: A railway passenger car invented and manufactured by George M. Pullman. More comfortable for day travel than the ordinary passenger car, it could be converted into bed sections for night travel. Later Pullmans were divided into roomettes, bedrooms, and compartments.

ROLLING STOCK: The wheeled cars owned by a railroad.

ROUNDHOUSE: A circular building housing idle locomotives and those needing repair. On the outside, in front, is a *turntable* to move them in and out on the proper track.

SECTION GANG: A crew of track workers employed to keep a certain section of track in good condition. They also weed the right-of-way, replace rotted ties, reballast, and raise sagging track.

SEMAPHORE: A mechanical arm with colored lights, used for visually signaling the engineer. The position of the arm during the day gave the signal: horizontal (red) for "stop" and vertical (green) for "clear— permission to proceed".

TENDER: A vehicle attached behind the locomotive for carrying fuel and water for the engine.

TURNTABLE: a rotating platform with a section of track long enough to hold a locomotive. It is used to reverse the direction of the engine or send it down another radiating track.

VARNISH: Wooden passenger cars, so called because they were lacquered to a shine.

WYE: A method of turning an engine around if there was no turntable. It was a turnout in the shape of the letter "Y" that by driving onto it, then backing up, got the engine running in the opposite direction on the main line.

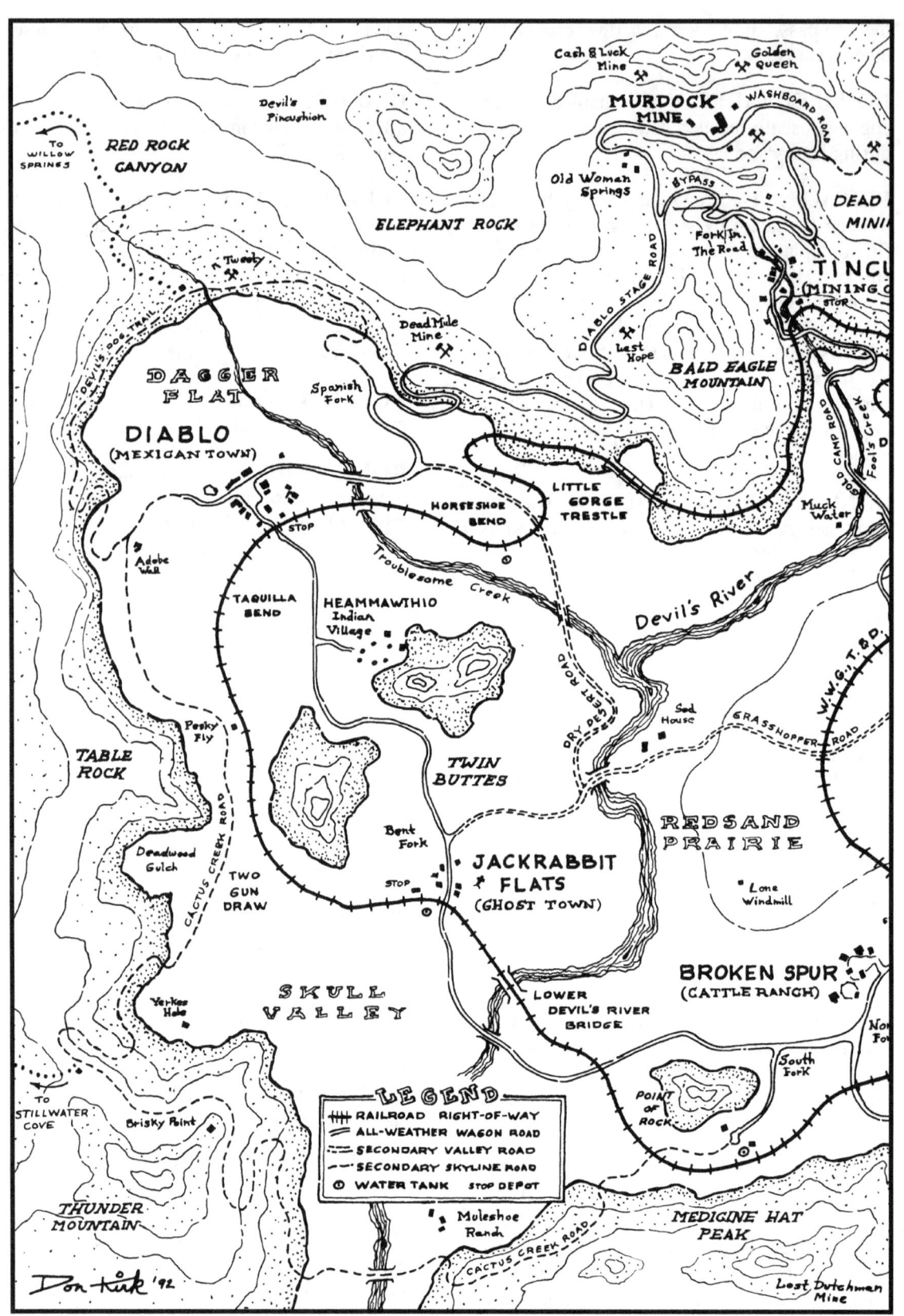

WESTERN HALF OF REDROCK CANYON TERRITORY

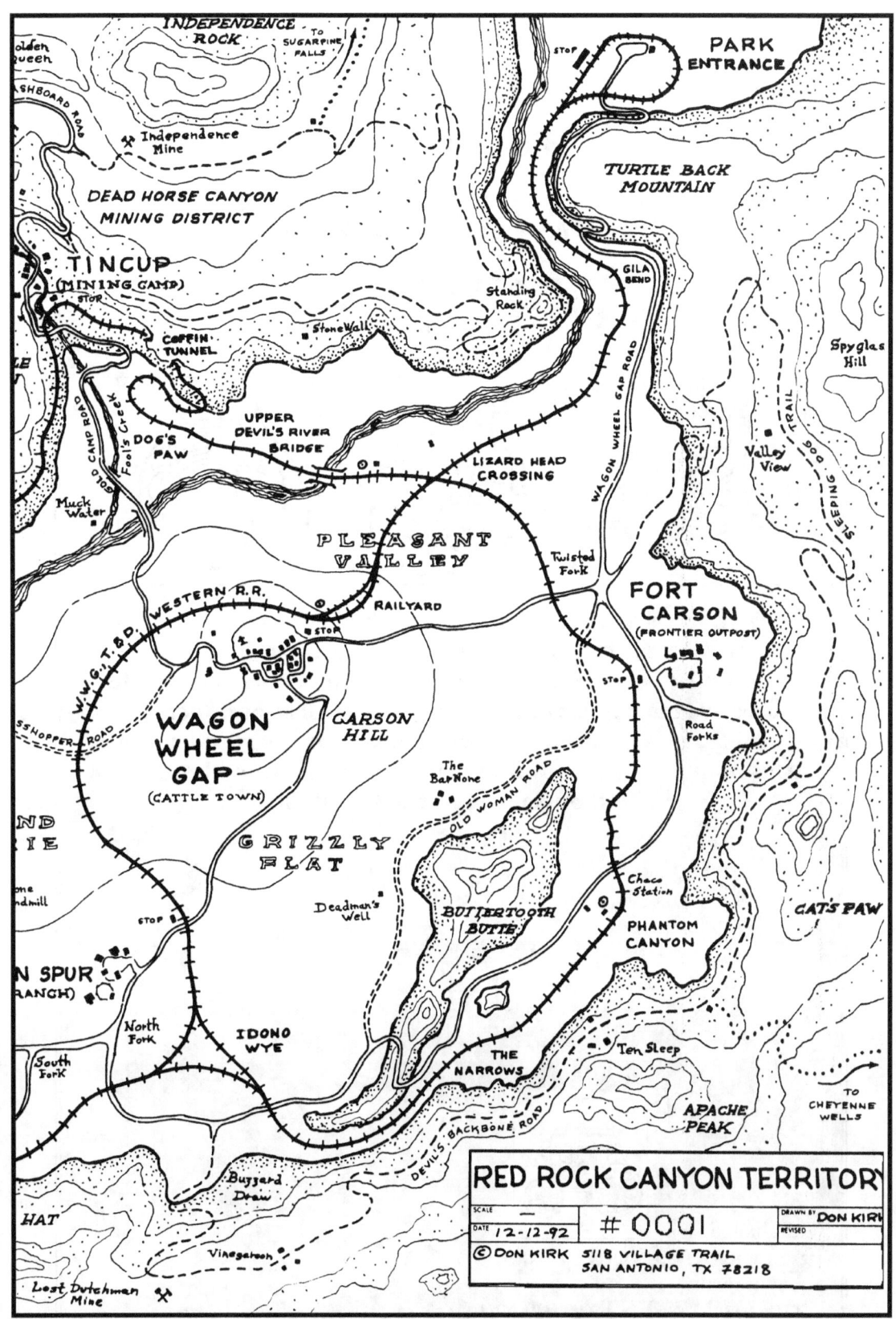

EASTERN HALF OF REDROCK CANYON TERRITORY

USA

Welcome To
REDROCK CANYON TERRITORY

  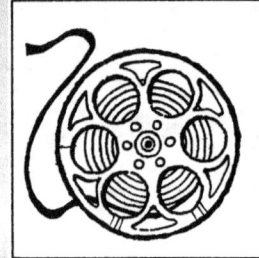

Originally written as a proprietary business proposal, it is now a popular manual that can be used as an aid in designing western-themed entertainment venues. It includes creative concepts, thought provoking ideas and facts to consider in developing western parks. For the western fan, this manual is chock-full of general information about life and businesses in the Old West.

"*RedRock Canyon Territory* is a dream world for western movie buffs and fans of the American West. Here they can take a trip to the past and explore all aspects of western popular culture through museum exhibits, books, films and entertainment of the period. The grandeur of the barren landscape and the rustic, weathered towns of *RedRock Canyon* envelop the guest in western fact and folklore. Guests step through the silver screen and find themselves inside the world of the Western movie."

Published by
SWEETWATER STAGE LINES
An imprint of
THE OLD WEST COMPANY™
San Antonio, Texas